TURBULENT TIMES LEADERSHIP

FOR SALES MANAGERS

TURBULENT TIMES LEADERSHIP

FOR SALES MANAGERS

HOW THE VERY BEST BOOST SALES

NEW YORK TIMES BESTSELLING AUTHOR

TOM CONNELLAN

TURBULENT TIMES LEADERSHIP FOR SALES MANAGERS
HOW THE VERY BEST BOOST SALES

Peak Performance Press, Inc.
1163 South Main Street, Suite 306
Chelsea, MI 48118
www.peakperformancepress.net

Ordering Information

To order additional copies, contact your favorite bookseller.
For a quantity discount on orders of more than 20 copies, call 800-344-5417.

ISBN 0-9769506-3-4 or   978-0-9769506-3-9 (trade paperback)

Credits

Developmental editing: Jeff Morris & Vanessa Mickan
Proofreading: Deborah Costenbader
Indexing: Linda Webster
Cover design/production: Michele DeFilippo, 1106 Design
Text design/illustration: Jeff Morris

First printing: August 2010

To sales managers everywhere,
because they're the ones who first proved
that these tools work well, work fast,
and produce lasting change.

CONTENTS

Preface vii

1. Three Keys to Improved Sales Performance 1
2. Believe in Them 9
3. Hold Them Accountable 29
4. Feedback: Get the Balance Right 45
5. Motivational Feedback: Use Reinforcement
   to Improve Performance 57
6. Informational Feedback: Use Sales Data
   to Motivate Your Team 75
7. Developmental Feedback: A Positive Approach
   to Nonperformance 87
8. Putting It All to Work 101

Three Powerful Ways to Accelerate, Deepen, and
   Sustain the Use of These Three Proven Tools 119

Have Tom Keynote Your Next Sales Meeting 125

About Tom Connellan 127

Acknowledgments 129

Index 131

Book Orders 136

PREFACE

This book is an outgrowth of what was originally a two-and-a-half-day seminar for sales managers based on my research, which is described in chapter 1. Over time, I learned what was needed to really make the tools work and was able to reduce the seminar to a day and a half—plus, for best results, some follow-on coaching.

Then, because the tools covered in this book produced positive outcomes for more than just sales managers, I started getting requests for presentations for leaders in virtually all functional areas, at all levels up through C-suite executives, and in virtually all kinds of organizations, including a wide variety of military functions, manufacturing, retailing, financial services, and software firms.

That led to *Bringing Out the Best in Others: 3 Keys for Business Leaders, Educators, Coaches, and Parents*, which became a *New York Times* bestseller.

But while some sales managers no doubt purchased that book and benefited from it, there was no book directed straight at the sales manager—the very individual at whom the content was originally aimed. It worked the fastest there because sales has a longstanding history of clear-cut metrics. It also worked well there because if you drive sales, you quickly drive the rest of the enterprise.

So, after talking to several publishers, a flock of sales managers, key people in publishing, my editor, and people to whom I have licensed the training materials, we decided that sales managers deserved a book of their own. It's never going to be a *New York Times* bestseller, because there aren't enough sales managers to create that much volume. It's not breaking new ground—I've already written about the research, the conceptual framework, and key processes—but the examples, applications, and specifics of what to do that I have given here are targeted directly at sales managers.

So, sales managers, here's your book!

CHAPTER 1

Three Keys to Improved Sales Performance

RICK IS A SALES MANAGER whose reps are getting exceptional results in a tough market. Unit sales are up, average order size is up, market share is up, customer sat scores are up, and margins are not only holding their own but are edging up.

But it wasn't always that way. Ten months ago, Rick and his team weren't doing so well in that tough market. They were fighting for every dollar of sales and discouraged by the results they were getting. The sales cycle was taking longer than it should. Market share and margins were both eroding. Customer sat scores were matching the all-time low. Reps were becoming dispirited and—in the words of HR—"not fully engaged in their jobs." In Rick's words, "some days they'd be firing on all eight cylinders and some days on about three. Way, way too often, I was waking up at three in the morning unable to get back to sleep. It was like riding a roller coaster with a lot more low points than high points, and it was driving me nuts."

The turning point came when Rick learned how to use three simple factors that got every rep on his team fully engaged, fully productive, and fully committed—three simple factors that I uncovered almost by accident and have since taught Rick and countless other sales managers how to use.

The next 117 pages are going to make your job easier and your results better, because whether you're in field sales, financial services, retail, or another function with a direct line of sight to revenue, you're going to learn how to use those same three factors that helped Rick boost sales.

What's the Secret?

I've been researching high performance for over 30 years now, and during one study, I uncovered a compelling statistical pattern. In looking at the backgrounds of high performers, I found that

- two-thirds of all entrepreneurs are firstborns;

- 21 of the first 23 astronauts were firstborns;

- 64 percent of the people from two-child families who are listed in *Who's Who* are firstborns.

There's a reason these data are of particular value to people interested in boosting the performance of people working for them—people like you. In the general population, firstborns—a group that includes children with no brothers or sisters—make up only 35 percent of the total.

The statistics intrigued me and made me dig deeper. Was this an adults-only phenomenon, or was it something that showed up in childhood? I searched out studies of children and educational achievement and found the following:

- In tests of nursery school, kindergarten, and day-care children, firstborns averaged 3.5 percent higher in creativity than later-born children.

- A ten-year study of 1,500 superior Wisconsin ninth-graders showed that 49 percent of them were firstborns.

- Over a 20-year period, 52 to 66 percent of entering freshmen at Columbia University were firstborns.

The deeper I dug, the more it seemed that firstborns were high performers in every field:

- A study of more than 2,000 military personnel showed firstborns are overrepresented in the higher ranks.

- Fifty-five percent of justices on the United States Supreme Court have been firstborns.

- A study in England in 1874 showed that firstborns were overrepresented among fellows of the Royal Society, England's national academy of science.

- Most female world leaders are firstborns.

- Over half of United States presidents have been firstborns.

- Most Rhodes scholars are firstborns.

Now I was more than curious about this pattern because it meant that an identifiable group of individuals accounted for a disproportionately high percentage of high performers across a wide cross section of academic, political, professional, and business groups. I began looking into what differentiated firstborns from the rest of the children. I read psychology journals. I talked with child psychologists. I interviewed parents. I watched families in action. I studied the life stories of astronauts, CEOs, Rhodes scholars, female world leaders, manufacturers, top students, military leaders, U.S. presidents, and others—such as the leaders of high-performing teams. I learned a lot.

> Most female world leaders are firstborns. Over half of United States presidents have been firstborns. Most Rhodes scholars are firstborns.

It turns out that parents are *unconsciously brilliant* in raising their firstborns. There are three ways parents treat their firstborns differently:

1. Positive expectations. Parents have more positive expectations for firstborns, because (everyone knows) they are the ones who are going to become the all-star quarterback, the president of the senior class, the captain of the cheerleading squad. A classic case of a self-fulfilling prophecy, perhaps, but it works to the child's advantage. In whatever direction the parents' expectations pointed, they tended to be higher for the firstborn.

2. Responsibility and accountability. Firstborns are given more responsibility than their peers, and at an earlier age. They're held more accountable. They're asked to look after and help take care of their younger brothers and sisters. When the kids go to the movies without adult supervision, the firstborn is given the cell phone and the money to buy tickets and popcorn, as well as the job of watching out for the younger ones.

3. Feedback. Firstborns get more attention, a faster response, and greater reinforcement from parents, relatives, and family friends. They have their pictures taken more often. Parents spend more time encouraging them to walk and talk, more time praising them when they do well, more time helping them overcome their failures (or even criticizing them, which is better than ignoring them, as we will see).

When I got to this point, I stepped back and looked at what I was uncovering. It was then I noticed something else: if you give a few seconds' thought to those three factors, you'll quickly see the same thing I saw.

You'll see that they are not genetic in nature. They are *environmental* in nature because they are not intrinsic but are instead external to the individual.

The simple fact that the factors are environmental led me to an interesting notion. What would happen if you recreated these three factors in another situation? What would happen if you taught leaders how to put the factors to work as a positive way of boosting the performance of the individuals on their team?

So I decided to conduct an experiment. I went to a company, told them what I'd found, explained that the three factors were environmental in nature, and asked if I could train some managers to use the three factors.

They gave me a group of manufacturing managers. I conducted a workshop on the three factors, did some coaching on implementation, and 90 days later, quality defects had fallen by two-thirds.

I went to another company, gave them the same explanation, and asked the same question. They gave me a group of sales managers. I spent two days with the sales managers, did some follow-on coaching to accelerate and lock in the impact of the training, and 180 days later—in a declining economy—sales had climbed from 80 percent of target to 133 percent of target.

> One hundred eighty days later—in a declining economy—sales had climbed from 80 percent of target to 133 percent of target.

Encouraged that I was on the right track, I tried the experiment in other organizations and in a variety of functions, including manufacturing, finance, sales, distribution, health care, research, and service organizations. The results supported my earlier findings. The three factors, when introduced into the work environment, can build a high-performance climate in almost any setting.

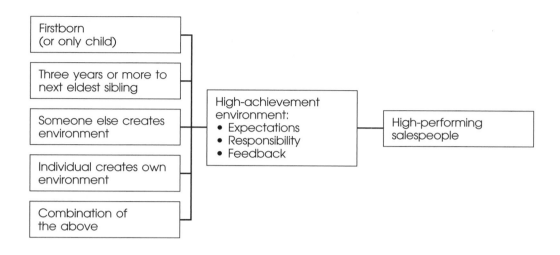

Sources of the environmental factors that make high achievers

Now, for those of you who are later born and are saying, "This guy is a little off, because I'm not a firstborn and I've done pretty darn well for myself," let me point out that the factors can come from a variety of sources. If, for example, there is an age gap of three or more years between a child and the next eldest sibling, it usually recreates the same environmental conditions all over again.

You can also create the three factors for yourself. That's frequently true for elite athletes. You may have created them for yourself, or a manager or mentor may have created them for you. One study I conducted of company presidents who attained their position before age 40 revealed that 67 percent could identify a mentor from earlier in their career who created the three factors in their job climate.

But the most important take-away for you is that you have the ability to use the three factors to boost the performance of your sales reps. For example, one of the most interesting studies I ran involved looking at the difference between high-performing sales teams and low-performing sales teams. I found that the managers of high-performing reps scored 22 percent better than managers of low-performing reps in their ability to put the three factors to work.

One way of looking at that 22 percent difference is to say that if you convert the research into street terms, the headlines of how to treat your reps are quite straightforward:

1. Believe in them.

2. Hold them accountable.

3. Give them supportive feedback.

Seems simple enough. Do you do those three things? Of course you do. Everyone in a leadership position does. We both know that. But even in the best of times, very few leaders use all three in a manner that *consistently* gets the performance levels they want.

If you look honestly at your own behavior, you're out of balance in some way—unless you're considerably different from every other sales manager we've studied or worked with, and I'd be willing to bet against that. In fact, *you'd* probably even be willing to bet against that.

- Some sales managers overdo accountability and underdo support. (This is the most common occurrence in normal times.)

- Some do the reverse—overdo support and underdo accountability.

- Some are flip-floppers. They overemphasize accountability, realize that's what they're doing, and then try to compensate by piling on the support. Then they flip back again.

- Others *say* they have confidence in their sales reps. But if we were to survey their reps, we might well get exactly the opposite answer— simply because while they're *trying* to express confidence, they're just not expressing it in a way that gets through to the reps.

- Some underdo all three factors.

In whatever way you're out of balance, it gets even more pronounced in turbulent times. As an example, if you tend to overdo the accountability element, turbulent times may lead you to hammer away even more than normal at accountability and slip even more on providing support. Not surprisingly, sales rep performance slips rather than improves.

In today's world you cannot be out of balance, you cannot flip-flop back and forth, and you cannot hold back. You need to do what the very best sales managers do:

You need to go *full throttle* on all three factors.

When you do, you'll start enjoying the same success as others who have put the three factors to work. Those attending the workshop on which this book is based reported, among other results, that their sales organizations had

- increased average line items per order from 6 to 11.2 on the inside order desk in a little under two weeks

- increased sales of higher-margin products

- boosted unit sales by 15 percent while maintaining the same average gross margin

- increased sales on targeted lines by 200 percent

- generated substantial volume in new accounts (in one instance, a high-performing sales rep accepted a challenge to call on five key accounts being supplied by a competitor; he switched three of the five, which added $2.5 million in new sales)

- reduced credits as a percent of sales from 0.86 percent to 0.74 percent (net annualized savings of $176,000)

More details about these results later. Right now, let's look at the three core skills you need to go full throttle on. Think of these core skills as a blueprint for getting full engagement from all your reps all the time.

1. Believe in them. You've probably heard of the self-fulfilling prophecy. A healthy dose of confidence helps us achieve our goals and leads to the greatest success. The same is true of your sales reps; when they feel your confidence in them, their performance will improve.

It's not enough just to have the metrics and goals; it's critical that you convey a high regard for your reps' knowledge, skills, character, and commitment. Once that's in place, it reduces anxiety and lets the reps focus on getting their job done.

2. Hold them accountable. Most metrics for sales are well defined. That's an important piece of accountability. Another chunk of accountability gets locked in during the goal-setting process. Yet another comes from any parameters that are set for how high or low the goals are. Set the goals too high and your reps will lose confidence they can achieve them, and motivation fades. Set them too low and they won't feel they need to expend much effort to achieve them. There's more about how to resolve those issues in chapter 3—including eight ways in which sales managers typically dilute accountability.

3. Provide supportive feedback. Depending on the type and amount, feedback makes the other two factors work really well or not at all. We've found it helpful to break feedback into its three primary categories—motivational feedback, informational feedback, and developmental feedback.

> Feedback makes the other two factors work really well or not at all.

Motivational feedback is mainly positive reinforcement—"applause"— and letting reps know how they're progressing. It helps keep them up, motivated, and moving ahead even in the toughest of times.

Informational feedback is about letting your reps know how they're doing. It's neutral in that it's simply information. A weekly or monthly printout of sales results is a form of informational feedback. And as you'll see in chapter 6, it's frequently misused in a way that reduces performance.

Developmental feedback is what happens when performance isn't where it should be. The phrase we use with our clients and in our workshops is "supportive confrontation of nonperformance." You have to confront nonperformance, and you need to do it in a manner that gets permanent improvement, not half-hearted commitment or that up-down-up-down-up-down roller-coaster performance that happens all too often.

Put these elements together and you'll have a set of tools that will

- maintain the stellar performance of your top performers,

- boost the performance of salespeople who are doing a good job but still falling short of their potential, and

- get salespeople and teams who are underperforming back on the right track.

If even one of those is of interest to you, let's get started by looking at how "believe in them" works!

CHAPTER 2

Believe in Them

IN AN ANCIENT GREEK MYTH, a sculptor named Pygmalion creates an ivory statue of the ideal woman and is so taken with its perfection that he falls hopelessly in love with it. His creation seems so real to him that he expects it to speak to him and return his love. He begs, prays, and offers it gifts. When it does not respond, he despairs. The goddess Aphrodite eventually takes pity on him and brings the statue to life.

Centuries later, the playwright George Bernard Shaw drew upon the Pygmalion myth to write the story of Professor Henry Higgins and Eliza Doolittle, an illiterate and uncultured Cockney flower girl. Higgins makes a bet with a colleague that he can train Eliza to speak in a cultured manner and pass her off as a duchess. Thanks to his positive expectations (and a lot of hard work), he eventually does so—and, of course, falls in love with her. Shaw's *Pygmalion* and the subsequent musical *My Fair Lady* dramatize Professor Higgins's success in using positive expectations as a basis for helping someone reach his or her full potential.

The Pygmalion Effect—the effect of one person's positive expectations upon the behavior of another—is alive and well in the modern world. It is a major factor in the best school classrooms and the most successful businesses.

"Smart Kids"

Perhaps no one has done more research on the impact of expectations than Robert Rosenthal, a former professor of social psychology at Harvard University. One of Rosenthal's more interesting studies was conducted in an elementary school with the help of Lenore Jacobson, a staff member of a West Coast school system. Each grade in the school had three classes: one for children of above-average ability, one for children of average ability, and one for children of below-average ability. Schoolchildren were given an intelligence test, which Rosenthal and Jacobson told teachers would accurately predict which students would become "intellectual bloomers." The researchers gave teachers the names of those children who, they said, had scored high in testing and would show remarkable gains in intellectual development during the school year. What the teachers were not told, however, was that Rosenthal and Jacobson had simply chosen 20 percent of the pupils, at random, to be "intellectual bloomers." The only real difference between these students and the other 80 percent in each class was in the minds and expectations of their teachers.

At the end of the school year, the children were again given the same IQ test. The children in each class who had been randomly designated "intellectual bloomers" showed an average IQ increase four points higher than their classmates—obviously the result of their teachers' expectations. When the teachers were asked to describe the behavior of their students, they said the "bloomers" were more interesting, more curious, happier, slightly more appealing, better adjusted, more affectionate, and less anxious for social approval.

> The children who had been randomly designated "intellectual bloomers" showed an average IQ increase four points higher than their classmates.

"Smart kids" lessons for sales managers

- Higher expectations lead to higher performance.

- If someone performs better than you expected, be aware that you *may* react slightly negatively. Avoid that.

- Don't pigeonhole people into being low performers. Not everyone can be great, but everyone can do better than he's doing now.

Also interesting was the way teachers reacted to students who improved in IQ but were not designated "bloomers": the higher their IQ gain, the more likely the children were to be considered less interesting, less well-adjusted, and less affectionate. Their improvement, against expectations, was viewed as a negative.

Aptitude vs. Attitude

Studies in the business world have produced similar results. Dr. Albert S. King worked with a group of underprivileged workers—former food servers, house cleaners, unskilled laborers, farm workers, and unemployed—enrolled in a worker training program to become pressers, welders, and mechanics. He selected 14 trainees at random and let their supervisors know that these trainees had "high aptitude potential" and could be expected to show unusual improvement and skill development. It's important to note that none of the trainees were told of this, and supervisors were also instructed not to reveal the information.

At the end of the program, supervisors were asked to rate each trainee's adjustment according to eight criteria. Sure enough, the "high aptitude personnel" (HAPs) rated much higher than the others. The consensus was that they knew more about their jobs, produced neater and more accurate work, learned new duties better, and were more responsible, cooperative, and logical. Their fellow trainees agreed; those considered the top performers and the best people to work with and be around were, as it turned out, those the researchers had, unknown to them, designated as HAPs.

HAPs lessons for sales managers

- Increased job performance can be instilled in anyone.

- Very small factors can drive huge shifts in confidence.

- Some of these factors are so small and so invisible that neither the sender nor the receiver knows the message is being sent.

- You may be totally unaware of some things you're unintentionally doing or not doing that could be destroying the confidence of your reps.

- Without becoming paranoid, pay attention to little things that can build your reps' confidence.

But the most interesting aspect of the study was its vivid demonstration of why the power of positive expectations is often called the Pygmalion Effect. The welders and mechanics were given practical and written tests over the course of their training. Those randomly designated as "high aptitude" scored significantly higher than the other trainees. The only plausible explanation was that the supervisors' high expectations had somehow influenced the HAPs.

Based on his observations, King concluded that supervisors probably revealed these positive expectations in ways so subtle that the trainees were not consciously aware of them. For example, twelve trainees—five HAPs and seven non-HAPs—were shown two photos of the same supervisor that were identical except for pupil size, which in one photograph had artificially been enlarged. They were asked (1) to state what, if any, differences they could see and (2) whether they saw any difference or not, to select the photo that showed how the supervisor usually looked at them. None of the trainees could articulate any difference, but all five of those the supervisor had been told were "high aptitude" selected the photo depicting the supervisor with enlarged pupils, while only two of the seven non-HAPs chose that photo.

> It was probably through eye contact that supervisors unconsciously signaled their positive attitude.

If they could not consciously discern the difference, why did the HAPs choose the photo with the dilated pupils? Psychological research has shown that large pupil size often indicates favorable attitudes and expectations, so it was probably through eye contact that supervisors unconsciously signaled their positive attitude to the HAPs. Although neither they nor the "elite" trainees were aware of how it was sent, the trainees got the message that they were superior performers and were expected to accomplish great things. The other trainees probably picked up on the same subliminal message and were cued to look more favorably on their chosen betters.

Works for Sales Managers, Too

In his classic *Harvard Business Review* article "Pygmalion in Management," J. Sterling Livingston described a similar response among sales managers. The district office manager of a large life insurance company observed that new insurance agents performed better in outstanding, fast-growing agencies, so he assigned his best agents to work with the best assistant manager. The six next-best agents were assigned to an average assistant manager, and the lowest producers went to work for the least able assistant manager. This distribution produced some interesting results.

1. The esprit de corps of the salespeople selected as the top performers— often called the "super staff"—was high, and their efforts were even better than anyone expected. Under the top assistant manager, they brought in an overall increase in sales.

2. The sales of the low producers, working with the lowest-rated manager, fell even lower than before, and as expected, attrition increased.

3. The average unit, which the district manager had expected to stay about the same, surprised Livingston by significantly increasing its sales. The assistant manager in charge of this group refused to believe that he was any less capable than the assistant manager of the "super staff" or that his agents were less capable than those in the top group. He communicated his high expectations to his sales reps and told them that with persistence and hard work they could match or surpass the performance of the "super staff," their strongest rivals. And in fact that is what they did: the "average" group increased their sales by a higher percentage than did the "super staff."

> The Pygmalion Effect is one of the strongest levers available to sales managers who seek to raise the performance level of their sales staff.

As this shows, the Pygmalion Effect is one of the strongest levers available to sales managers who seek to raise the performance level of their sales staff. But using this lever requires a certain amount of skill and finesse, which includes a familiarity with all of the factors that can affect expectations in the workplace.

You Can't Ignore Reality

Here's where too many sales managers go astray in this area: they confuse "believe in them" with wishful thinking. You can't solve problems by applying unfounded optimism. You can't just wish for improvement; you have to behave in ways that you know will lead to improvement. Positive expectations can and will improve the outcome when they are based on reality—that is, knowledge of the present situation and a firm belief in the steps that can be taken to improve it.

It's critical that you acknowledge the situation as it is, not as you would like it to be. If sales are down, own up to it. If you're getting squeezed on margins, tell people your margins are in a squeeze. If your industry is in a funk, acknowledge it.

Rather than saying, "Everything's great, and we're going to make headway over the next six months," you have to acknowledge current reality. Phrases like "We're 12 percent over budget on this," "The market is tight," "Our cycle time is 2.5 days more than it should be," and "Receivables are 18 percent higher than where we want them to be" all acknowledge current reality.

Believing in your team does not mean denying reality. It means acknowledging reality—usually with a brutal assessment of the current situation—and then creating a new reality.

> Believing in your team does not mean denying reality. It means acknowledging reality—usually with a brutal assessment of the current situation—and then creating a new reality by expressing positive expectations.

The way you create a new reality is by expressing positive expectations: "We're going to get things back on track." "We've got a strong team and we'll be able to overcome these temporary setbacks. It might take us three to four months, but we will get there." "In the next three days we're going to figure out how to be back on schedule by the end the quarter." "With the people in this room right now, we have the ability to get back on target within the next 30 days."

Put it all together and the model to follow goes something like this: "Things aren't going well now, but I know that you have the ability to get us back on track." This model acknowledges things as they are and starts creating the belief in a future reality that is better.

It also avoids confusing positive expectations with positive thinking. Positive thinking often becomes code for "Practice Pollyanna thinking and don't acknowledge reality." This misguided response to a turbulent marketplace is an all-too-common form of denying reality that makes you look foolish. Everyone knows what you're saying isn't true. Rather than admiring your optimism, they wonder if you've lost your marbles.

Describe the situation as you see it, and then drop it, except for discussions on how to overcome it.

Using the Placebo Effect to Jump-Start Performance

Everyone has heard of placebos—such as the inert sugar pills that used to be given to patients, who were told that the pill might improve their condition but not informed that the pill had no inherent healing effect.

Although this sham intervention is no longer used in today's medical practice because it's not considered ethical, it sometimes had a therapeutic effect simply because the patient *believed* the treatment would help.

You'll find it less surprising to learn that if your sales reps believe they will succeed, there's a much higher probability they will succeed.

We all know that customers don't buy because they're made to believe; they buy because the sales rep believes. The same thing is true of your sales reps. They don't believe in themselves because they're *made* to believe in themselves. They believe in themselves because they believe that *you* believe in them.

Notice that I didn't say they believe because *you* believe—although

> They believe because they believe that *you* believe.

that's an important first step. I said they believe because they *believe* that you believe. It's not enough that you believe in them. You have to demonstrate that belief in a way that they feel it. You have to

- say things that can instill that belief in them
- say those things in a way that will instill that belief
- use the right words
- use the right verbal intonations
- use the right nonverbal communications
- avoid interruptions
- use a setting that's conducive to what you're trying to communicate

In other words, you have to do everything you'd expect a rep to do when talking to a customer about your product or service.

But unless you're considerably different from every other sales manager we've worked with, you're not doing that. You're not doing it consistently, and you're probably inadvertently incongruent in some of the ways in which you communicate positive expectations. Because of issues like those, you're probably not having the desired effect on your sales reps. To illustrate, let's look at how a muddled message affected a manager named Mary.

Getting It Across

Mary walked in and threw down her pen. "That son of a bitch!" she muttered. "He has absolutely no confidence in me. He doesn't think I can do the job, and he puts me down every chance he gets."

Having witnessed Mary's discussion with Bill, her boss, I wasn't surprised by her reaction. Nonetheless, I asked her what Bill had said that made her feel that way.

"He said that he thought I was just the person for this type of project."

"So, what's wrong with that?"

"It's not what he said," she replied. "It's more what he *didn't* say and the *way* he said what he *did* say that made me angry."

Mary's reaction was a not uncommon one. How something is stated can be every bit as telling as the statement itself. We can communicate expectations, in particular, in a variety of ways, including both what we say and what we do. Even though the words he used were positive, Bill somehow communicated his expectations in a manner that made them seem negative. How did he do this?

When we try to communicate an idea to another person, we choose the words we think will best convey the message. The fact is, however, that most of the emotional content of our message is conveyed by other means—in particular, our tone of voice and our body language. It is also strongly affected by the environment in which it is communicated—the setting, distance between us, privacy, and other external factors.

This emotional content is an important—perhaps the most important—part of our message as far as the recipient is concerned. Why? Because expectations themselves are more about emotions than about cold, hard facts. This is not to say motivation is irrational, but neither is it rational—it is emotional, because emotion is what drives us to action.

If you are trying to communicate positive expectations to someone by using carefully composed positive sentences, you may think you're getting your message across. But if your tone of voice doesn't match the words, if your body language is awkward or defensive, if you're sitting far away from the person, if the chairs are hard, or if other people are continually entering or leaving the room, the message the other person gets is discordant, disturbing, and diametrically opposed to what you're trying to tell her.

It helps to have a system for scoring how effectively you're communicating your expectations to the other person. Based on the work of many researchers and combining it with what we know works, we've created a system for looking at how well someone communicates positive expectations. The first 80 percent of the impact is in the message itself, allocated like this:

Message	Impact Value
Words	5%
Vocal intonation	30%
Body language	45%

The other 20 percent of the impact comes from environmental factors:

Environment	Impact Value
Setting	10%
Proximity	5%
Interruptions	5%

The Message

Now let's look at these factors in greater detail to see how the message you think you're sending gets interpreted by the receiver.

The Words

A common misconception is that the message is carried entirely by the words. Yes, words are important, but in the final analysis, words carry only 5 percent of the total impact. Even so, word choice can be critical. The right word can make the difference that brings success; the wrong word can sink you.

When communicating expectations, use language that is appropriate to the individuals or group that you are addressing. "I anticipate success in this endeavor" might work for a group of university researchers, but it will get you laughed out of the room if you're talking to your sales reps.

Use positive words rather than negative words. Rather than saying "Don't forget the report," say instead, "It would be great if the report got here even before the deadline." You'll get a better response.

In general , phrase your message in positive terms rather than negative. The message is basically the same, but its impact is greater and more effective with the positive phrasing. Here are some other examples:

Instead of saying	Say
"Don't send in any more incomplete reports."	"Make sure all the sections are complete before you send the report in."
"Don't leave any money on the table."	"Make sure you get full value for the product."
"Don't leave the customer in limbo."	"Every customer question should receive a response of some type within one business day—preferably within two to three hours—even if it's just to say, 'I am looking into it right now and I'll have an answer by 9:30 tomorrow morning.'"
"Don't forget to thank the customer for the order."	"Remember the importance of thanking each customer for the order, and tell him you appreciate his business."
"Don't yell across the office that way."	"If you need somebody's help, walk over to where she is and speak to her in a normal tone of voice."

Vocal Intonation

"It's not what he said, it's the way he said it." Even the most positive, most pleasant, most innocent statement can sound like sarcasm, condescension, or abuse if said in the wrong tone of voice or with the wrong inflection. Words are 5 percent; we're giving vocal intonation a full 30 percent of the message's impact.

Let's look at this simple sentence: "I think Bill can do this." Innocuous enough, right? But there are ways of saying it that totally change its impact:

"*I* think Bill can do this." Implication: other people *don't* believe Bill can do this.

"I *think* Bill can do this." Implication: I don't *know* if he can do this; maybe he can, maybe he can't.

"I think *Bill* can do this." Implication: Bill can do it, but certain other people can't.

"I think Bill *can* do this." Implication: other people's doubts notwithstanding, I believe Bill can do it.

"I think Bill can *do* this." Implication: others think it can't be done, but I think Bill can pull it off.

"I think Bill can do *this.*" Implication: there's not much he *can* do, but maybe he can do this.

As you can see, *how* you say something makes a huge difference in how the message is received. And if you really want to deliver a positive message, say it in a way that leaves no doubt: "Bill's sharp, and he's experienced. He'll get it done on time and on budget."

Think I'm overstating my case here? Try the "Bill variations" above with your spouse or significant other—i.e., "I *think* you can do this" or "I think you can do *this*"—and see how it goes over.

Body Language

An enormous amount of unspoken information is conveyed or implied by how we sit, stand, gesture, and position our bodies while we're talking. For this reason, we're counting it as 45 percent of the message's impact. If your body language conflicts with your spoken message, your intended message may be totally lost. There are five primary categories of body language:

- body position

- gestures

- head position and movement

- facial expressions

- eyes

All of these categories must work together to reinforce and support your words and vocal intonations. You can say the right things with the right intonations but still fail to get your message across if your body language is incongruous with the message.

Body position. An open posture, facing toward the person you're speaking to, helps communicate positive expectations. Sit or stand straight and lean forward slightly.

One way to inadvertently communicate low expectations is to close off your body position: turn your body away from the individual, cross your legs, and fold your arms. Another term for this is the "cold shoulder," and on the next page you can see why.

I have conducted (and videotaped) hundreds of role play interviews with sales managers participating in our training programs in which we discussed job performance. I played the role of the sales manager and each of them played the role of a sales rep whose performance had slipped. At the outset of each interview, I would deliberately assume this aversive posture. All but a few responded quickly with similar body language—looking away from me, crossing their legs, folding their arms, edging farther away. They also began responding in a negative way in their discussion—becoming defensive, irritable, and slightly hostile.

The cold shoulder

Then I would ease into a more relaxed, open, positive posture and use more eye contact. Within moments, the individual playing the sales rep would respond with positive body language of his own, as well as with a more positive tone in his spoken responses.

He would begin to suggest ways he could improve his performance—a huge difference from moments earlier when he was defensive and had nothing to offer but empty excuses.

After that demonstration, there was never a shred of doubt in the sales managers' minds about the effects of spoken language and body language on their sales reps' responses.

Gestures. People communicate a lot with their hands. Clenched hands or fists are seen pretty much for what they are: hostile gestures. Tapping your fingers on the desk signals impatience. Don't hide your mouth, wag your finger, or point at someone you're talking to. Gestures like these communicate negative expectations, no matter what you're saying in words.

To build trust, keep your hands open. This signals openness and honesty. Touching your hands to your chest, resting your hand palms down on the tabletop, and "steepling" (elbows on table, hands raised, fingertips touching) are gestures that tell the other person you're paying attention, you're confident, and you have confidence in him.

Facial expressions. People in conversation with one another are highly attuned to facial expressions; these are the most readily identifiable elements of body language. Positive expectations are best communicated with a smile, a relaxed mouth, and general alertness. If you've got a tight jaw, a grim smile, or raised eyebrows, you're signaling distrust or disbelief.

Eyes. The best way to communicate positive expectations is with your eyes wide open and your pupils dilated. The former you can control; the latter is an involuntary response, as we saw in Dr. King's studies. A lack of eye contact goes against your positive message; it makes the person you're addressing feel unimportant, even unwelcome. You should also be careful not to squint or appear to be looking down your nose at people.

The table below summarizes how body language affects the communication of performance expectations. Most of these are intuitively obvious;

Effects of body language on communicating performance expectations

	These communicate positive expectations	These communicate negative expectations
Body position	Open Erect Leaning forward	Arms crossed Legs crossed away "Cold shoulder"
Hand gestures	Open hands Steepling Hand to chest Touching	Tapping fingers Hiding mouth Wagging finger Closed or clenched hand
Head	Straight Nodding	Shaking side to side Tilted Bowed
Face	Smiling Mouth relaxed Alert Attentive	Frowning Tight-lipped Jaw clenched Grim smile Raised eyebrows
Eyes	Wide open Eye contact Pupils dilated	Narrowed No eye contact Pupils constricted Looking down nose

you know from personal experience which gestures and facial expressions are off-putting and which are welcoming and positive. At the same time, I can assure you that, without realizing what you're doing, you sometimes use one or more of the types of body language that communicate negative expectations. And since we both know that it's not what message you intend to send but what message is received that counts, I'd ask that you be sensitive to your body language, become aware of which of these you're unconsciously using, and then work to change your behavior.

None of the above is intended as a step-by-step guide to communicating positive expectations. If you are feeling positive toward the person you're speaking to, your gestures, your body language, your tone of voice will naturally be positive and will support and reinforce your words. But unless you're the world's best actor, you can't speak positive words that you don't mean and accompany them with manufactured gestures indicating positive expectations; you have to mean it. When you don't mean it, your listener will know.

Unfortunately, the opposite is not true. You can mean it, but if all the elements we're covering here are not congruent, your sale reps won't experience your belief in them.

The Environment

The remaining 20 percent of your message's impact is carried by factors external to the message. We consider their cumulative relative importance to be 20 percent, allocated as follows.

Setting

The best place to communicate high expectations to an individual is in a physical setting that makes her comfortable. This means downplaying the supervisor-subordinate relationship as much as possible; you need to convey that you're in a neutral situation where you can discuss matters frankly and on a relatively equal footing. A good setting contributes about 10 percent of the impact of your message.

Your office can work as the setting if you arrange things properly. Don't sit behind your desk with the other person seated in front of it; this unnecessarily emphasizes the boss-subordinate roles and is useful only if there are issues to be negotiated and you wish to retain an edge by demonstrating or emphasizing your rank in the company. Instead, for a relaxed, friendly discussion, have her sit beside your desk, or even better, beside you at a table where you can examine documents side by side. By arranging things this way, you're saying, "In this situation, we're pretty much equals. And because I'm comfortable with my position, I'm going to sit next to you so we can talk about this reasonably. I'm doing this because I have great confidence in you."

Arrangement is an important factor in group settings as well. If you're seated around a conference table, say for a team meeting, make sure people are seated evenly around the table, not bunched up at opposite ends (see A in figure at right). If there aren't enough people to fill the spots, group everyone toward one end. You can do this by placing a chart or a display monitor on the table so that everyone has to sit together on the viewing side of it (B). This fosters a team spirit and draws everyone into the conversation. It also avoids inadvertently creating a feeling of division, an "us against them" undertone, that can insinuate itself into a group in subtle ways.

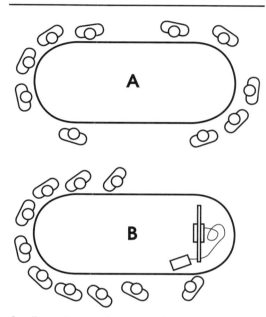

Seating at a conference table

Proximity

Each of us has a certain amount of personal space. Sometimes we guard that space against unwanted intrusion; sometimes we invite people in. The amount of space we need depends on the degree of intimacy we want or expect in a given situation. Anthropologists recognize four personal space zones that encompass us like the layers of an onion. For most of North America, the distances are generally as follows:

- **Intimate.** This zone is the space within 18 inches of us. It's for our closest relationships: lovers, parents, and children. It's not for business relationships. We can skip this one.

- **Personal.** The space from 18 inches to about 3 or 4 feet around us is used for one-to-one conversations; the outer limits can also be used to communicate positive expectations to another person.

- **Social.** Three to twelve feet from us is the zone most of us use for business and for discussing things in a small group setting. As a rule, the closer you position yourself to the three-foot distance, the more positive your communication can be.

- **Public.** From 12 feet on is the space you use for addressing large groups—large company gatherings, user groups, association meetings, shareholder meetings, or outside groups such as the PTO.

Positive expectations could be communicated to high performers in any of these zones, but for our purposes we'll limit our discussion to the personal, social, and public zones, where most business is conducted.

The personal zone. This is where most one-to-one interactions are conducted, where you begin to establish the spirit of working together as a team. By sitting down beside the other person to examine a sales report, you're implying that the two of you are partners sharing a mutual concern. Close up, the effects of facial expressions, small gestures, and eye contact are maximized.

The social zone. Team meetings and other types of conferences operate in the 4- to 12-foot interpersonal zone. Here, nonverbal communication—hand gestures, head movements, etc.—needs to be a little more pronounced. The "sweet spot" is the near distance, closer to the 4-foot interval, where your positive expectations are communicated most powerfully. For this reason, leaning forward toward the person you're addressing can increase the effectiveness of your message.

Suppose you're sitting with several sales reps around a table. If you want to persuade Natalie, across the table from you, that she can indeed snag that key account, you can lean toward her, put your elbows on the table with your hands steepled in front of you, look her straight in the eye, and say, "Natalie, I *know* you can get this new account. Dealing with this type of buyer is your forte, and with your experience and ability, I don't see any reason you won't get this account on board sometime in the next 60 days—maybe even a small beginning order on the first call."

The public zone. If you're talking with more than a few people at once, you're probably communicating in the public zone. Gestures need to be somewhat exaggerated here—hitting your fist on a podium, throwing your arms wide to emphasize a point—to carry the same weight as smaller gestures do in more intimate situations. A pep talk to a large group is more a performance than a conversation, so you need to exaggerate your movements and your speech, almost as an actor would on a stage.

Of course, you need to avoid using this technique if you're addressing small groups or individuals. Communicating positive expectations works better close up. Don't use the public zone if you can avoid it, especially if it's in your office. For example, if you've invited three people in for a chat, don't seat them at the far end of the office and stay behind your desk as if in a fortress (see A in figure at right). Instead, invite them all to sit around your desk (B), or better still, join them around a table away from your desk (C). This fosters a feeling of collegiality rather than superiority and inferiority.

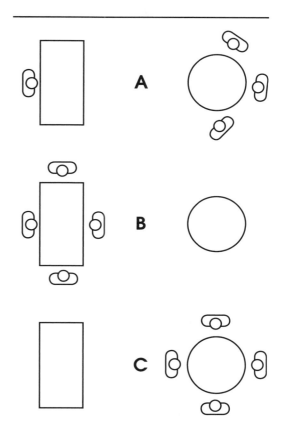

Seating for a conference in your office

Interruptions

In communicating your confidence in a person and giving him a message that you expect him to accomplish great things, make sure he truly is the most important person in your office. This means don't tolerate interruptions. Don't take phone calls, don't let people to come in and engage you in conversations, and especially don't leave the office "just for a second" to handle an emergency (unless it's a true emergency). Give the person your full, undivided attention. To do otherwise is equivalent to telling the individual, "I consider this phone call (or chatting with the boss, checking e-mail on my BlackBerry, signing this letter, shuffling these papers) more important than the important matter I asked you in to discuss." Yes, perhaps the Blaine Soup

Factory account is more important, but it's also true that Chauncey Q. Blaine III can be told you're in a meeting and that you'll get back to him just as soon as the meeting is over.

To forestall interruptions, ask that your phone calls be held, then stick to your resolve, no matter who calls, unless you're absolutely sure it's a real emergency. Close your office door, and if anyone knocks, ask him to wait or tell him you'll call him later. Of course, a closed door often is a signal that the person visiting within is about to get chewed out, so tell your visitor up front what the meeting is about. Reassure him that the discussion is going to be friendly and that you want to avoid interruptions so you can devote your entire attention to the issue. This will put him at ease and make him more receptive to your message of positive expectations.

If you can't avoid interruptions in an office setting, move the discussion somewhere else—a cafeteria, a restaurant, a conference room—where you can talk face-to-face, uninterrupted and undistracted, for however long you need.

Bill and Mary Revisited

With what you've just read fresh in your mind, let's go back and reexamine what happened when Mary and Bill had an unproductive conversation.

Words. What Bill said was, "I think you are just the person for this type of project." Positive, right? But Bill didn't say why she was ideal. He could have been more specific about her experience, her training, her skills, her background in market research. However, this wasn't the critical factor in the misunderstanding.

The crucial issue, as it turned out, was his use of the word "person." Mary told me, and it was confirmed by others, that Bill used this word only when assigning tasks to women; with men, he used other phrasing, such as "You're just the one for the job." On his word choice, we'll give Bill a decent score, but not the highest—say, 60 out of a possible 100.

Vocal intonation. Bill stressed the word "this" in his statement to Mary: "I think you are just the person for *this* type of project." The subtle message, which he swore he didn't intend to convey, was that Mary was perhaps unsuited for other types of projects—a blow to her confidence and motivation. Bill gets only a 10 for this faux pas.

Body language. I was present when the conversation took place, and here's what I observed. Bill was standing with his arms crossed, his body turned slightly away from Mary—giving her the "cold shoulder." Although his hands were not clenched, they did remain firmly clamped on his arms. With his head tilted up and slightly away, he was looking down his nose at her. He would pat Mary on the back now and then—the way you might pat a child on the head—but then immediately recross his arms, as if to take back the gesture. His only facial expression was a grim, tight-jawed smile. He spent most of the conversation looking away from Mary rather than straight into her eyes. Overall, the impression he gave was one of condescension. Bad, bad form. Score: 10 out of 100.

Setting. The discussion took place in a busy hallway. Not unusual, but not very conversation friendly, either. Let's give him a 40.

Proximity. Bill propped his foot on a box, which he kept between himself and Mary. This put him three or four feet from Mary, the outer edge of a comfortable conversation zone. Score: 40.

Interruptions. One after another, people kept walking by, and Bill interrupted his conversation with Mary to greet and smile at each one. Once he even stopped to sign a requisition form. Six interruptions in two minutes. If you were Mary, how would you feel? Score: a flat zero.

Rating Bill's conversation with Mary

Message (80%)	Bill's Score	Impact Value	Net Score
Words	60	5%	3.0
Intonation	10	30%	3.0
Body language	10	45%	4.5
Environment (20%)			
Setting	40	10%	4.0
Proximity	40	5%	2.0
Interruptions	0	5%	0.0
		Total Score (out of 100):	**16.5**

As you can see, Bill didn't score very well. And no wonder. He scored high on only one factor—words—but words count for only 5 percent of the total picture.

Fortunately, Bill soon learned—and you will, too—that top performers thrive on a carefully conceived and thoughtfully delivered communiqué. In the office and out, both medium and message can make or break the power of positive expectations.

The one important thing that runs through this chapter but has not yet been stated explicitly is that *everything matters*. Everything! Every word, every gesture, every tweak to the setting. Every one of those must be congruent with you and your message. Every one must advance the strategic intent of your firm.

For the best performance from your sales reps, think, "I'll see it when I believe it."

Your job is to communicate—in every aspect of your communication—your confidence in your sales reps in such a way that they *experience* that confidence. Improvements in *their* performance begin with changes in *your* behavior.

You've heard people say, "I'll believe it when I see it." Well, in bringing out the best performance in your sales reps, we advocate a slightly different mindset: "I'll see it when I believe it."

When you start believing in a way that pierces your reps to the core—putting to work everything in this chapter—you'll start seeing the initial shifts in behavior within 24 hours. Once you have that initial momentum underway, you merely have to keep it going, and as you'll see, that's easy with the tools in chapter 5.

CHAPTER 3

Hold Them Accountable

IF ANY FUNCTIONAL AREA has a history of metrics and measurements, sales would be right at the top of the list. Among the most commonly used metrics in sales are

- dollar volume
- unit volume
- gross margins maintained
- new accounts opened
- account penetration
- customer satisfaction
- customer retention
- market share
- growth rate
- closing ratio
- average order/ticket/basket size

The names vary in actual use, but the core measurement remains the same. The financial services industry, for example, uses return on assets as a key metric; retail generally uses some version of average basket size; restaurants monitor average ticket size and daily or weekly sales. And since anyone with a direct line of sight to revenue is a 3.0 Sales Manager, front-line managers in at least those three industries are sales managers.

You'd think that with as many metrics as sales has, who's accountable for what wouldn't be an issue. But that's not always the case. Although the core metrics for holding a rep accountable are almost always in place, the ways in which the core metrics are implemented often dilute their power. There are eight common ways in which the pure power of accountability normally associated with good metrics gets diluted:

1. Agreement on the metric but not the actual goal

2. Agreement on the metric but adding a little to the goal

3. Activities getting labeled as goals

4. Goals not balanced against tradeoffs

5. Flip-flopping between high goals and low goals

6. Using the "automatic rubber band"

7. No action plan backing up the goal

8. Goal-setting period too long

We'll talk about each of these in detail and look at what you can do to avoid making these mistakes with your sales staff.

1. Agreement on Metric But Not Actual Goal

Everyone may agree that dollar volume is a key metric, but there may not have been enough thorough discussion to lock in on a goal with which everyone is fully engaged. Here's a way to check whether you and your reps are in complete alignment. On a single sheet of paper, answer the following questions about one (or all) of your reps:

1. What metrics are you using to measure his performance? Use the above list as a starting point. Then add, delete, and modify so it's 100 percent accurate as you see it. If you're in financial services, for

example, you probably don't use gross margin as a metric, but you probably do use return on assets.

2. Prioritize them in a rough order of importance.

3. For each indicator, identify the level of performance you expect, and identify the date by which it should be achieved.

Once you're answered these questions for yourself, ask the rep (who isn't aware of your responses) to answer the same questions from his perspective. That is:

1. What metrics does he think you're using to measure his performance? Have him use the above list as a starting point, and then ask him to add, delete, and modify so it's 100 percent accurate as he sees it.

2. Have him prioritize the metrics in a rough order of importance.

3. For each indicator, ask him to identify the level of performance he thinks you expect, and identify the date by which it should be achieved.

Now sit down with him and compare lists. How closely do they match? If you're a typical sales manager, there will be some daylight between the two sets of answers. It happens whenever there hasn't been a thorough discussion on goals from the start and then ongoing discussions about priorities, resources, and marketplace conditions.

We've tested this mismatch in our programs—usually at the behest of a sales manager who insists that everyone is in alignment at her company. It's a fairly simple test. We ask the sales manager to list a sales rep's metrics

> The degree of difference between your view and his view of his goals is a pretty good indicator of how far off his potential he is performing.

and the goals associated with each metric in order of priority on a flip chart page. Then the sales manager simply calls, shoots an e-mail, or texts the sales rep, explaining the point under discussion and asking him to respond with a list of his metrics and goals for the specified period. When they come in, we put them on a flip chart page. Then we simply compare the two lists.

They never match. The numbers are different. The priorities are different. (Any item that is within one ranking we give credit as being the "same," even though that's not precisely the case.) Dates are different. There are usually a couple of activities disguised as goals on both the sales manager's list and the rep's list. Naturally, there are usually different activities on each list.

Now, if that holds true with your rep, how valid is your appraisal of that person's performance? How can the rep achieve goals that he's unsure of? The degree of difference between your view and his view of his goals is a pretty good indicator of how far off his potential he is performing. Exhorting this person simply to work harder doesn't do much good. He may work harder, but toward the wrong goals or toward vague, uncertain goals, leading to more frustration for you, the company, and the rep.

Now consider this. If your responses to the above test don't match your reps' responses, what's the probability that you and your boss's responses don't match? Actually, pretty good. We've run some 8,500 pairs of matched interviews over the years testing that idea, and we've found about a 25 percent failure rate in matching up the responses between a manager and that manager's direct reports.

So check the matchup with your reps, and check the matchup with your boss. Think of it this way: If you and your reps don't match, they're getting stabbed in a duel they don't even know they're in. If you and your boss don't match, *you're* getting stabbed in a duel you don't even know you're in.

If you and your reps don't match, they're getting stabbed in a duel they don't even know they're in. If you and your boss don't match, you're getting stabbed in a duel you don't even know you're in.

Think about the implications of that 25 percent failure to agree. If you put 100 percent of your energy into your job as you perceive it and there's that 25 percent gap, what's the highest you can get on a performance evaluation? About a 75 percent score. Chances are pretty good that some version of that has happened to you at some point. Chances are also pretty good that some version of that has happened to your reps at some point.

Don't let either of those events happen again. Get 100 percent alignment, starting today.

2. Agreement on Metric But Pushing Goal

Carlos was a regional sales manager who always added a little to all of his direct reports' targets just to make sure that everything got accomplished.

That's not an uncommon practice, but as is the case in too many companies, it was compounded by the fact that everyone else in the chain of command was doing the same thing.

The vice president of sales and marketing was adding a little. So was the director of sales. So were Carlos's seven district managers. By the time targets got translated into individual territories, they were far enough out of reach that they generated more complaining than initiative on the part of the sales reps.

If you're adding a little to make sure you reach your budget, you're going to find out that—because the tools in this book work—you can make your budget (and then some) without sneaking in a little safety factor.

3. Activities Labeled as Goals

First, let me acknowledge that you may use a term other than "goal" for the end result you want accomplished. Some companies use "objective"; others use "goal" for longer-term results and "objective" for shorter-term results, or the reverse; still others use "target." The terminology is unimportant; it's the process that matters. I'm going to use "goal."

That said, "I want you to improve communications" is a worthy and laudable intent. But it's not a goal. Neither is "You need to find more prospects that have higher potential."

If the goal doesn't include one of the metrics at the beginning of the chapter—or something equally solid—then it's probably an action step that's going to help reach a goal attached to one of those metrics.

You can get a vague feeling that communication has improved, but you have no way to measure it. If it's anything, it's a poorly stated action step that is intended to help you accomplish a goal. "Calling" on someone isn't the goal. It's what happens *after* the call that is the core of the goal: a new account, increased sales, increased margin, increased customer satisfaction, or any of a host of metrics.

So avoid as goal statements like these, because they're all activities:

- "Improve communications."

- "Coordinate with marketing."

- "Hold regular meetings."

- "Update the customer files."

- "Implement new call plan."

Instead, think of them as action steps a rep may take to accomplish a goal that reads something like this: "Generate at least $215,000 in new account business from accounts that have a gross potential of at least $1 million a year by October 10 without affecting volume from present accounts."

If the goal doesn't include one of the metrics at the beginning of the chapter—or something that is equally solid—then it's probably an action step that's going to help reach a goal attached to one of those metrics.

4. Goals Not Balanced Against Tradeoffs

Any goal becomes more attainable if you're willing to sacrifice something else. You can sell a lot of product if you sell it cheaply enough, but you won't make any money. You can generate a lot of business from new accounts, but you might find that takes too much time away from current customers, which can lead to lost accounts or lower account penetration. You can cut past-due accounts by eliminating credit, but you'll drive off a lot of responsible, loyal customers.

For this reason, every stretch goal should identify the limits of any tradeoffs. For instance, "Increase unit volume from an average of 220 a week to an average of 245 a week by June 30 *without reducing margins more than 1.4 percent.*" This puts limits on how the goal can be attained, which makes it harder, but it forestalls damage to other vital measures of performance.

A better way to state goals is to identify any tradeoffs that exist or that you're willing to live with.

The participant in one program confessed that his company had failed to do that and it had cost them dearly. Corporate had set a goal to increase sales by a significant amount. That naturally trickled down to the individual reps, who read the numbers they had been given, looked at the product line, and quickly made a very easy decision.

The product that was the easiest to sell had one of the highest prices and the lowest margins. The reps mentally shrugged. "If volume's what they want, I'll give it to them," they decided, and off they went. They sold that product like mad. Sales went up, overall margins went down, and profitability suffered accordingly.

A better way to state goals is to identify any tradeoffs that exist or that you're willing to live with. Here's an example: "Increase sales from an average of $315,000 per month to $350,000 per month in the next 90 days *without decreasing gross margin more than 3 percent.*"

This goal statement specifies an end result; it's realistic; it has a completion date; it's under the control or direct influence of the rep; and the limits of any tradeoffs are clearly identified.

5. The High Goal/Low Goal Flip-Flop

Vanessa was a district manager participating in one of our sales manager boot camps. She had six reps reporting to her, with one open slot that she was actively interviewing for.

Two of her reps were overly competitive with each other. Competition sometimes seemed to help performance, but usually it simply led to a hyper-competitive atmosphere, which was more destructive than constructive.

The other four were Marie, Will, Sue, and Josh. With these four, Vanessa had tried both high and low goals. She noticed that lower goals helped them feel successful, but then Marie and Will pretty much stopped trying when they reached that point. She also noticed that although setting higher goals motivated Sue and Josh, Marie and Will got discouraged because they didn't see any way to hit those goals.

> When it comes to motivating a sales rep, which works better, high goals or low goals? The answer is yes.

Vanessa was at a loss about whether to set high goals or low goals, so she asked a reasonable question: "When it comes to motivating a sales rep, which works better, high goals or low goals?"

My answer was yes. Here's why.

A goal should include some stretch, which forces people to improve their skills, but still be within reach. Stretching for an impossible goal leads only to frustration and disillusionment. "Double our sales this year" is probably an unrealistic goal; "Increase revenue by 1 percent over the next 18 months" is too easily attainable and therefore not a stretch.

The highest motivation occurs when the goal is midway between trivial and impossible (see figure on next page). If the goal is too easy and success is a slam dunk, sales reps are simply not fully engaged and may even lose interest

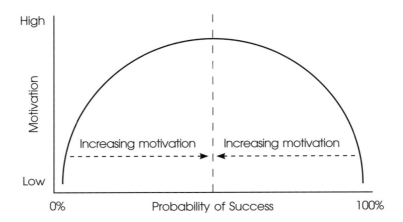

Probability of success vs. degree of motivation

in the goal. On the other hand, if it's obviously impossible, engagement is also zero; what's the use?

Full engagement occurs when there is a moderate probability of success but also some risk of failure if the effort is less than vigorous and committed.

The key factor in turning the individual into a high performer is that the sales rep must be in control of, or have direct influence over, many or most of the variables that make the goal attainable. Under these conditions, setting stretch goals leads to increased motivation, faster learning, greater skill improvement, and higher performance. Without control or direct influence, salespeople have no real hope of achieving success by their own efforts.

How high should goals be set? As we said, they should be high enough to stretch the individual's abilities but not so high as to be impossible. A good way to gauge the correct level is to use the "min-max" or "standard-goal" approach.

When a goal is stated as a single number, it is often seen as a win-lose, reward-or-punishment measure. It tends to be used as simply an evaluation and punishment tool rather than a growth and development tool. It doesn't allow for honest effort or for circumstances beyond the employee's control: either you make the goal, or you're a loser. This may generate the adrenaline of fear, but fear is a stressor, not a good long-term motivator.

Suppose a sales manager sets a goal for a sales rep to bring in $500,000 in sales in the upcoming quarter, and the rep brings in $477,000. Not bad, right? Too frequently, a sales rep who falls short, even if only by a little, is reprimanded or given a low evaluation at the end of the year with the accompanying impact on compensation. The rep quickly learns to view goals as punishment rather than opportunities for growth.

You respond: Okay, we don't want to be unduly harsh or punitive, but on the other hand, we don't want reps or anyone else wallowing in mediocrity or complacency. That's right, which is why we recommend that you consider, where you have the option, setting goals that afford a range of satisfactory achievement—the "standard-goal" approach.

This type of goal has two levels: a lower level that is a minimum or "passing grade," and a higher goal that represents an ideal, a goal to strive for, an "A plus." The lower goal is used for evaluation; the upper goal is to encourage growth and development.

Here's how it works. Suppose you and Dorothy, one of your sales reps, agree on a standard of $450,000 and a goal of $500,000 in sales for the next quarter. The standard is low enough to be achievable by a competent sales rep who is performing at an acceptable level. Achieving $450,000 in sales is enough to let her keep her job and salary. The higher level, which is called the "breakthrough goal," is high enough to be a stretch. To reach $500,000 in sales, Dorothy will have to work extra hard, use all her skills, sharpen a couple of them, and perhaps even learn a couple of new skills.

At the end of the quarter, having brought in $477,000 in sales, Dorothy has not reached her breakthrough goal but has comfortably surpassed the standard, the minimum requirement. As Dorothy's supervisor, you can now tell her one of two things:

- "You missed your goal by $23,000," or

- "You exceeded the standard by $27,000."

Which is better?

You'll get a better result praising her for exceeding the standard. Other companies have found that this approach fosters growth and motivation. It encourages the employee to set a higher target the next time around. Here's how you make that happen. You tell Dorothy: "The standard for this quarter was $450,000. We set a stretch goal of $500,000, and you hit $477,000. That's pretty darned good, you have a definite trend line up, and you're on the way to setting a new personal best. I have no doubt you'll do even better next quarter. Let's talk about the upcoming quarter."

This technique works in several ways:

- It makes it more likely Dorothy will operate at the top of her motivation curve.

- Rather than being committed to a single target, you and Dorothy can consider a range of expectations, which is more realistic in a world where conditions change from day to day.

- It encourages Dorothy to set higher stretch goals, because she knows she won't get beat up for being too ambitious if she misses.

Think of these as "Gotta Get" and "Gonna Shoot For" levels. The rep has to hit the lower number and is going to shoot for the higher number.

Can you use standard-goal, min-max, Gotta Get/Gonna Shoot For all the time? Maybe, maybe not. Maybe your company system is set up so that it's not an option. But sales managers who use it when and where they can—maybe even by keeping the goal the same and agreeing that the goal will be reached by May 1 and that the rep will shoot for reaching it by March 15—report that it works well for them.

6. The Automatic Rubber Band Effect

Ideally, you want the rep to set goals for himself that require extra effort to achieve and are therefore occasions for growth in skills and smarts. Stretch goals are like moving up to the next level in weight training: you set a goal that you may not be able to reach yet but which you can strive for and eventually achieve, and you grow stronger in the effort.

Stretch goals are like moving up to the next level in weight training: you set a goal that you may not be able to reach yet but which you can strive for and eventually achieve, and you grow stronger in the effort.

But stretch goals can be counterproductive if misused. Suppose, instead of praising Dorothy for topping the standard by $27,000, you express disappointment that she fell short of her stretch goal by $23,000, or that she sees her evaluation suffer as a result. What's her likely response? She will do everything she can to lower her goal so that she has a better chance of achieving it and getting a better evaluation at the end. With lower expectations come lower motivation and less incentive to work hard. Her sales will slide, her performance evaluation will slip further down, and the next goal will be set even lower. The result is a discouraged sales rep, poorer results, a loss of motivation, even poorer results the next time—a race to the bottom.

The idea behind stretch goals, of course, is to achieve the opposite of this result. You want reps to raise their sights, not lower them. That's why you set the threshold standard and count anything in between that standard and the higher goal as a positive. Surpassing the standard becomes an occasion for nudging both the standard and the stretch goal a bit higher every time.

So the question becomes: How fast do you raise the standard when Dorothy's performance consistently exceeds the standard? In my experience, the

> Surpassing the standard becomes an occasion for nudging both the standard and the stretch goal a bit higher every time.

standard must be raised, but not automatically as soon as she hits a particular level of performance. She managed a respectable $477,000 in sales, beating the standard by $27,000. If you respond by raising the minimum to $495,000, you create a figurative rubber band that snaps her in the posterior. She'll remember that, and the next time she's asked what the new stretch goal should be, she'll remember that snap and think: "Maybe this time I'll try to beat the standard by only $10,000, so my stretch goal will be $460,000. That will give me some breathing room." Thus, you're teaching her that the low-risk route is to take shorter and shorter steps, defeating the purpose of stretch goals.

Avoid the rubber-band effect. Instead, use a sliding scale. If Dorothy beats the standard by $27,000, let her know you're pleased with her progress. Consider leaving the standard at $450,000, but ask her what she thinks her stretch goal should be next time. If you've done a good job of bolstering her confidence, she will respond by raising her sights. If she continues to exceed the standard by more each time, it's reasonable to keep nudging the standard higher, but never so high that a slight dip in sales will cause her to fall out of the range of expectations.

This is a safe, reasonable, and comfortable way to continually raise expectations and motivations at the same time. You're always able to say three things to Dorothy about her job performance:

- "You've exceeded the standard, and you're doing a good job of meeting the basic expectations,"

- "You're continuing to improve," and

- "You're capable of higher achievement, so let's set a breakthrough target you can shoot for in the coming months."

7. No Action Plan Backing Up the Goal

Goals are not worth much without an action plan to achieve them. This action plan must focus the sales rep on the "how"—that is, what actions need to be taken to achieve the goal.

This doesn't mean your reps should end up with 10 to 12 pages of routine activities they carry out. What it means is that they should have a list of the three to seven stretch goals they've committed to and a list of the primary steps they need to take to accomplish those goals. Maybe that's half to a full page of action steps for the several goals that require significant stretch, significant involvement of other functional areas, or significantly different skill sets than were previously required.

By way of example, if we tie this back into several of the metrics from the beginning of this chapter, it might look something like this:

Metric	Gotta Get	Gonna Shoot For	Needs Detailed Action Plan
Dollar volume	$450,000	$500,000	
Unit volume	132	143	
Gross margin	23.5%	24.2%	X
New accounts	2	4	X
Percentage of customers who would definitely recommend	60%	68%	
Number of lost accounts	0	0	
Average order size	$3,200	$3,550	

In this example, two metrics require an action plan—gross margin and the number of new accounts. They don't have to be complex, and they sure better not be long—maybe a page for each one.

Here are seven guidelines to make sure that your reps' action plans will lead them to the right goal every time:

1. Set up checkpoints. Reps need checkpoints at certain steps along the path to their goal so they can change their behavior if they fall behind target. These checkpoints let reps know their progress and whether they need to speed up, slow down, revise, modify, delete, or add steps to the plan. Thus, the goal can be met even if the conditions change.

2. Be specific. The action plan steps need to be stated clearly and be measurable, so that reps can tell when they have completed them successfully. "Implement new call plan" isn't nearly as clear as "Implement new call plan by February 12." And while "Improve communications" isn't useful, "Get 100 percent buy-in from affected departments by March 26" is.

3. Hold them accountable. It is important to note specifically who is accountable for each step that must be taken to reach the goal.

4. Give the plan stretch. Just as goals should stretch reps, action plans must stretch them, too, because action plans consist of the steps necessary to accomplish the goals. These steps should force reps to learn new skills, try out new behaviors, and grow in some way on the job.

5. Don't stretch reps too far. A good action plan helps your reps learn how to be more effective at tackling future challenges and problems. But if you make the steps too difficult to achieve, it's like throwing them into the deep end when they haven't learned to swim. They may become discouraged about their problem-solving abilities and hesitate to confront future problems that they probably could solve.

When your reps write an action plan down on paper, it increases the probability that they will think it through properly, that other people will become involved in the action plan, and that the goal will be reached.

6. Write down all the action steps. Frequently, sales reps set overly ambitious goals and don't think through the action steps necessary to reach them. The sorry results? Missed goals and frustrated sales managers. But when they write an action plan down on paper, it increases the probability that they will think it through properly, that other people will become involved in the action plan, and that the goal will be reached.

7. Develop a contingency plan. Once a rep has laid out her action plan, ask her what might go wrong and prevent her from completing it. Ask how she would know that something had gone wrong—and if something does go wrong, what can be done about it? Fostering this thinking in your reps helps them come up with contingency action steps that can be taken if conditions change—for instance, if a major supplier goes on strike, a major customer goes bankrupt, or some other disaster.

8. Goal Setting Period Too Long

When the world is upside down, you need to shorten the goal-setting period. What corporate needs to run the company is not what you need to motivate your reps. Corporate may be using yearly targets, but what you need is weekly or monthly targets—maybe even daily targets.

How do you determine what the right goal-setting cycle is? Look at the natural rhythm of things. For one industry, it might be weekly. For another, it might be monthly.

One firm knew that equipment demos led to equipment placements and equipment placements led to product sales. Although the demos-to-placement ratio varied by rep, the range was pretty tight: depending on the rep, two to four placements occurred for every ten demos. Product sales naturally flowed from having the equipment in place. Reps received a base plus a commission based on product sales.

Sales managers set weekly demo goals with reps and asked the reps to break that down into daily targets. They combined the accountability with expressions of confidence in the reps' ability to hit the targets, added the supportive feedback techniques that are covered in chapters 4–7, and enjoyed the 12 percent boost in sales that resulted—all in the middle of the toughest economic environment since the 1930s.

> Sales managers combined accountability with expressions of confidence in the reps' ability to hit the targets, added supportive feedback techniques, and enjoyed a 12 percent boost in sales—all in the middle of the toughest economy since the 1930s.

You can enjoy similar benefits because you now have the tools to create a powerful foundation of accountability that will build strength of character and strength of purpose. Without accountability for specific goals and the action steps necessary to reach those goals, your reps will require enormous amounts of time and energy on your part because they'll never learn to manage themselves and you'll have to be right on top of them 24 hours a day. With accountability built in, they'll spend more time managing themselves, which means you don't have to constantly look over their shoulders. Do yourself a favor and get the basics in this chapter down pat.

Combining "believe in them" and "hold them accountable" gives you a solid base. Once you've laid that base, how do you keep your reps performing at a higher level? By harnessing the power of feedback—so let's see how that works to bring out their very best performance.

CHAPTER 4

Feedback: Get the Balance Right

NOW THAT WE'VE COVERED the importance of positive expectations and accountability for improving your sales team's performance, it's time to lock in the final piece of the puzzle—feedback. But for most, feedback is a word that's used in many different ways.

"I gave her a little feedback on exactly what I thought of that comment!" has one meaning.

"Could you give me a little feedback on this?" has another meaning.

So does "Obviously, he took the feedback to heart."

And if you think back to the chapter "Believe in Them," you can change the meaning of these statements as many times as you change the word you emphasize. As an example, compare:

"I gave her a little feedback on exactly what I thought of that comment."

vs.

"I gave her a little feedback on exactly what I thought of *that* comment!"

vs.

"I gave her a *little feedback* on exactly what I thought of that comment."

They each have different meanings. With the word "feedback" used in so many ways by so many people, let's look at how the very best sales managers use feedback to boost sales. It turns out that they break feedback into five different categories:

1. No feedback

2. Negative feedback

3. Motivational feedback

4. Informational feedback

5. Developmental feedback

To understand the impact of the five types of feedback on your reps' motivation levels, imagine you are at a neighborhood party. Someone told you the most hilarious joke that morning—every time you think about it you nearly crack up—so you take a deep breath and tell it.

First, picture yourself delivering your punch line, then waiting for the laughter and applause—but being greeted with silence. The faces of your audience are expressionless, and after the briefest of pauses they pick up their conversations exactly where they left off, as if you hadn't said anything at all. You feel demoralized. No one thought enough of you to even respond, and now you feel disrespected, disappointed, and a bit confused, uncertain what to do next. That's because you've just experienced the least-motivating type of response: *no feedback.*

Now imagine that you give your all to telling the greatest joke ever, and on wrapping up, you are greeted by grimaces and groans. One woman even says, "Why on Earth did you tell that joke? It's just not funny at all." That's *negative feedback.* If you're like most people, you turn ten shades of red, and you feel pretty irritated by those humorless killjoys. You may even get a momentary urge to "show them" by telling another joke. If that one fails, too, you'll probably stop trying (to the great relief of the party's host, no doubt!).

Okay, now rewind and picture another scenario. Your timing's great, you nail the punch line, and then you look from face to face, and everyone's laughing. One person pats you on the back and says, "You're the best"; another tries to get some words out but can't stop laughing. You feel elated, and for a moment you wonder if you could have been a stand-up comic after all. This is *motivational feedback.* Feels good, doesn't it?

What if you could get a more objective measurement of your performance? Well, it turns out that your company's head of market research is at the party. She helps you out by surveying the guests on their reaction. This gives you the humor equivalent of customer sat scores, and with this *informational feedback,* you have a clearer sense of how well you performed and whether you need to change your delivery the next time you tell the joke.

Finally, let's imagine that you were smart enough to bring along a joke coach to the party. When those humorless guests groaned at your joke, you'd have had the support of your joke coach to help you get back on track. He would have taken you aside to talk about the problems with your performance and where you could improve in the future; he would have given you *developmental feedback.* Even when you did a good job of telling the joke, he could help you improve your performance so you could do an even better job of telling that joke, or any other joke, in the future.

Feedback at Work

The people on your sales team are no different. They respond to the different types of feedback just as you would. So let's take a look at each type.

No Feedback

When a sales rep receives no feedback at all for his performance at work, it's known as *extinction,* because there is no encouragement for him either to continue behaving in that way or to change. It leaves him feeling drained and in limbo, uncertain how to behave next. Think of a halfback running down the field who's met with absolute silence from the fans on the sidelines. Absence of feedback is the least motivating kind of feedback you can give.

Here are some sales-related examples of no feedback:

- A rep who for several months has only just been meeting his targets tries a new strategy in his sales calls and sees a 5 percent increase in volume, yet his sales manager doesn't say anything.

- A rep consistently meets her targets and reporting deadlines and helps mentor newer reps whenever she can. Her sales manager is glad to have someone so reliable on the team but doesn't let her know that.

- A sales manager notices that one of her reps has been increasing the amount of time spent calling on high-potential accounts (which is part of their agreement from 45 days ago) and while pleased by the effort, doesn't say anything to the rep.

Negative Feedback

Negative feedback is *punishment,* such as when you adopt a negative manner to tell someone she's fallen short of your expectations. You may yell, throw your hands up in exasperation, or become very agitated or irate. In the case of our football player, his team's fans may boo if they think his progress down the field isn't good enough. If done exactly right, negative feedback has the potential to be energizing in that the result may be a renewed effort to perform better—but not always, and only for the short term.

Examples of negative feedback:

- A rep e-mails in a report two days late and with some of the information missing. His sales manager shoots back a blistering e-mail, with a copy to the VP of sales, questioning the rep's skills, motivation, and commitment to the firm.

- A rep who had been underperforming at identifying potential new clients puts in extra hours and finds five high-value potential accounts to call on. Her sales manager says, "So what? Your gross margin is still down this month."

- At a meeting, a rep runs through a new sales presentation he has prepared, and his sales manager responds by frowning and shaking her head.

Motivational Feedback

Motivational feedback is the reinforcement people receive when they've done a good job or shown improvement—say, when a rep lands a profitable new account and you text her a congratulatory message or are able to look her straight in the eye and tell her the same thing. Or both: you text her immediately, and the next time you see her you mention it again. You can think of this type of feedback like the crowd clapping and cheering on the sidelines at the football game; it boosts our halfback's confidence and spurs him on toward the goal line. Motivational feedback is called *reinforcement* because it strengthens good behavior and makes the person more likely to repeat that behavior.

Good motivational feedback looks like this:

- Saying to a rep, "You're getting better and better at your pre-call planning, Emily, and it's showing up in your results. I really appreciate that extra effort on your part."

- Sending an e-mail to a rep: "Alex, I noticed that you're spending more time working some of the higher-potential accounts that are tougher to land. Keep persevering, because we both know it will pay off in the end."

- Mentioning to an experienced rep, "Drew, I just wanted you to know that the time you spend helping develop some of the newer reps is really appreciated."

Informational Feedback

Then there is the concrete feedback you give your staff—figures and charts showing growth or decline in dollar or unit volume, accounts, gross margin, customer satisfaction, or other metrics. This informational feedback gives them an objective measurement of how they're doing. Think of it as the line markers on the field: our halfback needs those to gauge his progress toward the goal line.

Below are some examples of informational feedback:

- A rep accesses daily, weekly, monthly, and YTD sales online.

- You e-mail a copy of an industry report to all your reps.

- Each rep gets a quarterly report of dollar volume for each product, by account, that includes a rough estimate of what the full potential is for that product in each account.

Developmental Feedback

There will inevitably come a time when a sales rep fails to perform at the level you need, and that's where developmental feedback comes in. This is when you discuss his lack of performance and how it can be improved. In our football analogy, this might be the coach taking aside the halfback during a practice, working with him on a specific skill set, and then being sure to give him motivational feedback during practices and games to make sure the behaviors stick.

Here are three examples of developmental feedback:

- "Eleanor, I noticed your volume has dropped by about 15 percent over the last four to five months, and I'm concerned about that because I know you're much better than your sales results currently show."

- "Marie, your last three reports have been about a week late, and I'd like to talk with you about getting them in on time."

- "Thomas, in looking at the sales report, I see that you're pretty consistently missing the agreed-upon demos, and that's a critical element in our strategy. I know you can do it, so let's take a look at how we can get those demos up to where they should be."

The Pitfalls of Extinction and Punishment

Extinction (no feedback) and punishment (negative feedback) are in most cases the least effective ways to motivate your reps to improve their performance. Regarding extinction, if you ignore someone's bad performance as if it didn't happen, it is likely to be repeated or grow worse. If you make no response to someone's good performance or improved results, you haven't done your part to make sure that improvement continues. He put in extra effort to improve, but you didn't recognize it, so if you don't care, why should he?

Some sales managers use negative feedback when performance has improved but not as much as desired. They might say, "Sure, you're doing better at identifying potential new customers, but you've got to do a lot better to get your sales up to where they should be." Sometimes this works, but more often it only makes the sales rep feel as if she's being punished for trying—and people who are consistently punished for trying will eventually stop trying.

We want you to focus on the three types of feedback that are the most effective at improving reps' performance—motivational, informational, and developmental feedback—so the next three chapters will be devoted to each of those in turn. Before that, though, we want to give you some key advice about the least-motivating types of feedback—extinction and punishment—to help you avoid the traps that other sales managers too frequently fall into when giving feedback to their team.

1. Avoid the most frequent feedback mistake most sales managers make. All of us like attention. If we can't get good attention, then we'll (usually unconsciously) settle for bad attention. The thing we find hardest to accept is no attention. What a manager should be doing is giving reps positive attention (reinforcement) for the kind of behavior that improves results, and minimizing the amount of attention reps get when they do their job poorly (extinction).

Yet too many sales managers often do the opposite: they are overattentive and quick to criticize when someone messes up. Worst of all, many say and do nothing at all when a rep does something well, performs reliably all the time, or shows improvement.

A classic example is when an underperforming sales rep starts to lift her game. For instance, after weeks of prodding, a rep finally starts taking the initiative to make sales calls on her own to big, potentially lucrative accounts. The sales manager's tendency is often to think, "Well, she's finally started doing something right." Rarely does the manager go to her and tell her that she's making progress in the right direction. Without reinforcement, she loses motivation and slowly stops making the extra effort required to prepare for and make those really tough calls.

> Most sales managers know the difference between reinforcement and punishment, but close to 87 percent are woefully unaware of the devastating impact extinction has on sales performance.

Extinction—the least motivating type of feedback—is the most common type of feedback sales managers give for improved performance. Most sales managers know the difference between reinforcement and punishment, but close to 87 percent are woefully unaware of precisely how powerful extinction is and the devastating impact it has on sales performance.

Watch yourself over the next 30 days and see how many times you're missing the opportunity to reinforce someone who has improved his performance, helped out a colleague, made a valiant effort that didn't pay off this time, gone out of his way to maintain positive relationships with marketing communications, or done any of the hundreds of other things that we so often forget to reinforce from time to time. Each of those is a time you unintentionally extinguished that behavior, thereby reducing the probability that behavior or a similar behavior will occur in the future.

2. Punishment often backfires. Perhaps the biggest disadvantage of punishment is that it frequently backfires on us. It has unintended and often undesirable side effects. Moreover, what we intend as punishment or embarrassment frequently ends up being reinforcing. I see a clear example of this several times a year. I frequently have the opportunity to address sales meetings on the topic of "Creating Exceptional Customer Experiences." Often there are awards given out, and sometimes my schedule is such that I'm there when awards are made. Too frequently, the sequence of awards might go something like this:

"The first award we want to give out tonight goes to Dave Gregory. Dave received the largest single order from any customer during the course of the year. Dave, come on up and receive your award." (Loud clapping and cheering while Dave receives his award.)

"The second award of the evening goes to Kathy King. One of Kathy's accounts did more dollar volume with our company than any other account this year. Kathy, come up and receive your award." (Loud clapping and cheering for Kathy.)

"This third award is given each year to the individual who had the largest percentage increase in sales over last year. The award this year goes to Karen Revill. Let's have a big round of applause for Karen as she comes up to receive her award." (Loud clapping and cheering for Karen.)

"Now, this last award is given out each year to the person who's been late to more sales meetings than anybody else over the past year. It's designed to encourage him or her to be on time during the coming year. The award this year goes to Pat Burns." (Loud clapping and cheering while Pat walks up to receive his award.)

Pat is being unintentionally reinforced for the wrong behavior. All that clapping and cheering probably represents more attention and reinforcement than Pat normally receives. Clearly, the intention was to punish Pat, to embarrass him into coming to the meetings on time, but the probability of his being late the following year is actually increased rather than decreased. It's no surprise to me when I learn that the same people have won it year after year. And why not? Winning it gives Pat more attention than he's had all year, and, rather than being ignored, he'd prefer *some* attention, even negative attention, over no attention at all.

3. With punishment you often end up shooting the messenger. Just as everyone who works for you deserves to be told the truth, you need to hear the truth yourself, whatever it is and wherever it comes from. To achieve great results through thick and thin, you have to know the situation, including the bad news. And when the bad news is brought to you, remember: don't shoot the messenger by yelling at that individual.

"Well," you say, "when the news is bad, I do get angry." That's understandable, but if you take out your anger on the bearer of the news, you're only ensuring that (1) the individual will do almost anything to avoid bringing you more bad news; (2) there will be more bad news, but you won't get it; and (3) because you don't have a complete set of information, you'll make some lousy decisions.

Don't scream and shout and moan and throw papers on the floor. Your message to the messenger should be to thank him for his courage in bringing you the bad news. If you must show anger, show it in your work, your laser-like focus, your determination to set things straight. Your people want to know there's a mature adult in charge, not a spoiled, self-absorbed rock star.

When the messenger gets shot, you may find that productive behaviors get eliminated also. Let's look at a sequence of events to see how this happens.

1. A sales rep makes an error on a competitive analysis report, which is later forwarded to the VP of Sales.

2. Approximately two weeks after making the error, the rep notices the error on his own.

3. He reports his error to his sales manager.

4. The sales manager berates the rep for making such a dumb mistake.

5. The rep learns not to report his mistakes to the boss.

Too frequently, we "shoot the messenger" in our organizations. When we discipline the bearer of bad news, people learn quickly that it doesn't pay to deliver such news. That's why so much information at the top of an organization is filtered or edited. When the upper levels of an organization receive filtered, late, or incomplete information (good information with bad parts left out), they start making poor decisions. Yet we managers frequently have no one to blame but ourselves because we're the ones who started the "shoot the messenger" syndrome.

There is a way to use a rep's admission of an error as a teachable moment, and we'll show you that in chapter 7.

4. Beware the illusion that punishment has long-term positive effects. Although punishment frequently works in the short run, it almost never works in the long run. People get used to punishment, and after a while, it has relatively little effect on their behavior. Just as yelling has little effect any more on a child whose parents yell at him frequently, reps likewise become used to punishment from their manager.

A second disadvantage of punishment is that it doesn't teach new skills or behaviors. If you yell at reps, you will probably get them to stop what they're doing wrong, but you may or may not get them to do what's right. If you also yell at them to start doing something, they'll probably make a run at doing whatever that something is, but they may or may not do it the way they're supposed to.

The only way you can get someone to learn and practice new skills and behaviors is to demonstrate your confidence in their ability to learn the new skill set, make clear what you're going to hold them accountable for, and then provide lots of reinforcement for the progress they're making.

The third big problem with punishment is its unpredictability. Determining exactly how people are going to react to negative feedback is difficult, and we often find ourselves getting the wrong response, perhaps even the exact opposite of the one we wanted. Sometimes people will fight back directly. Other times, they will fight back indirectly; we can't see them retaliate, but they eventually stymie us with another bizarre behavior pattern. It might take days, weeks, months, or even years, but people who've been punished have subtle—and not so subtle—ways of getting back at those who dished out heavy doses of punishment.

The very best sales managers know the pitfalls of negative feedback and failing to give feedback at all, and use them judiciousy in the few situations where they work. They prefer to use a balanced mix of motivational,

> Determining exactly how people are going to react to negative feedback is difficult, and we often find ourselves getting the wrong response, perhaps even the exact opposite of the one we wanted.

informational, and developmental feedback—delivered in the right form, at the right time, in the right words and tone.

In our workshops, we often meet sales managers who think they are doing a good job of providing feedback and can't understand why they aren't getting stellar results. The reason is almost always that they're thinking of feedback in general terms rather than specifically in terms of the three most useful for boosting sales performance—motivational, informational, and developmental.

One workshop participant told me that he decided to take action on a recommendation he'd received a couple of months earlier from one of our coaches. He asked his team members to lock themselves in a room for a few hours and figure out what they wanted him to do, do differently, or stop doing altogether to help them perform better.

When they told him they wanted more feedback, he was shocked: "I send them industry reports; I pass along market information from headquarters; I forward relevant e-mails to them. If anything, I thought I was overloading them with feedback.

"But what you just said about different kinds of feedback opened my eyes," he told me. "They didn't want more *informational* feedback. They wanted me to let them know they were appreciated. They wanted me to acknowledge their progress. They wanted me to notice the extra effort they were putting in on some really tough accounts.

"In short, they wanted more *motivational* feedback!"

In the next chapter we're going to look at how you can use the power of motivational feedback to boost performance and sales in your team.

CHAPTER 5

Motivational Feedback: Use Reinforcement to Improve Performance

LET'S TAKE ANOTHER LOOK at our football player. When he's gaining yardage, the most likely feedback from his team's fans is that they will clap and cheer wildly. And when they show him their approval, it makes him feel good and encourages him to continue the behavior that won their approval: to run as fast as he can toward the goal line.

The same idea applies in your sales team. Positive feedback is your applause, your cheers for the rep, and it can take many forms—a congratulatory phone call or quick text when he shows great persistence and nabs a new account, or maybe just walking over to his desk to tell him you appreciate an improvement in the way he identifies potential new customers. Your positive feedback strengthens—reinforces—that behavior and makes him more likely to repeat it.

Reinforcement is energizing. It validates the rep's efforts. It lets him feel he's accomplished something and makes him want to achieve even greater things. Everybody has experienced this, and everybody knows it works. That's why the best leaders use reinforcement whenever they can.

In the previous chapter, we touched on the dampening effect that "boos" and "silence" can have on sales performance. Now we're going to look at how you can use the "cheers" to boost sales performance.

What the Best Sales Managers Know About Reinforcement

The behavior you want from your sales reps covers a whole range of actions that boost sales. It might include anything from planning their sales calls well, calling on the right customers, and identifying customer needs, to asking for the sale frequently enough on sales calls. The key to getting your team consistently performing the way you want is reinforcement—acknowledging them when they do it right.

Once you get the desired behavior pattern going in your reps, it takes only a small amount of reinforcement to keep it going.

Once you get the desired behavior pattern going in your reps, it takes only a little reinforcement to keep it going. The behavior will become a habit, and a habit is like a car: it takes a bit of energy to get the car moving, but once it's rolling down the highway, it takes a lot less energy to keep it going. Of course, if you stop giving it gas altogether, it will eventually stop rolling.

The same principle holds true with your sales reps. You need to put in some time and extra reinforcement at the beginning to get them up and running, but once they're there, you can maintain their performance with just a little well-timed reinforcement. And if you stop giving your reps reinforcement altogether, they too will "stop rolling."

What Type of Reinforcement Works Best?

There is no single answer to this question, because reinforcement has to fit the time, the place, the event, and the person. Reinforcement that's appropriate in one situation may not be at all appropriate in another situation or for another person.

Reinforcement is not all hearts and flowers and just being nice to people. It's about giving your team members feedback that makes them want to keep repeating the right behavior. This means that you need to put yourself in a rep's shoes and give feedback that you know he will perceive as positive.

You also have to adapt reinforcement to your personal management style and to the field you work in; otherwise it will seem unnatural, and your team may end up suspicious of your motives. In certain sales environments, it might be appropriate to say, "David, I truly appreciate all the hard work you're putting in, and it's really great that you just made that big sale. Good for you!" But if the sales manager is a retired Marine with a reputation as a no-nonsense straight shooter, a combat-hardened veteran who now runs a team selling heavy equipment to the construction industry, talk like that won't cut it. He would sound more sincere if he said, "Dave, you might be the ugliest guy in the room, but you wouldn't know that from your sales this month. You rock!"

Reinforcement Is Crucial in Turbulent Times

In theory, it may seem that a paycheck should be reinforcement enough for your sales team, especially in a tight economy when there is less job security. You are paying them to do a good job, so why should you go out of your way to compliment them for doing what they're getting paid to do?

Let me answer that with another question: Are all members of your team generating profitable sales in substantial volume and doing everything they should be doing, such as prospecting, getting lots of referrals, looking for ways to further penetrate new accounts, analyzing competitors' strategies, keeping client information files up to date, carefully planning each call, turning in all reports on time, and putting in that extra 10 percent of effort that makes a difference at any time but especially when the economy is tight?

No?

I didn't think so. Chances are, some of those areas could do with at least a little improvement. Yet these sales reps are still getting paid. So, effectively— from a behavioral point of view—*at least some members of your team are being paid for poor performance.*

You may not like that statement. Most sales managers don't. Most HR directors don't. Most CFOs don't. Truth is, no one likes that statement.

But that's exactly what's going on.

Don't feel like the Lone Ranger. It doesn't happen just with your team. It happens in most other companies and elsewhere in yours. No manager intentionally pays people to do mediocre work, but that's what happens in many organizations: people are, in essence, reinforced—paid—for not performing well at some part of their job.

> From a behavioral point of view, at least some members of your team are being paid for poor performance.

Clearly, then, other forms of reinforcement are crucial for motivating your team to boost sales. Luckily for you, sales reps do not live by bread alone. *Psychological income* can be just as important to them. A major contributor to psychological income is the reinforcement you give them when they perform well or show improvement. In those situations where companies cannot offer dollars and perks the way they used to, psychological income has an even greater role to play.

I know reinforcement works, because I've even seen it boost sales among commissioned salespeople. Since they are paid only when they make a sale, you'd think that they would already be as motivated as they could be. But when sales managers have learned the importance of reinforcement and begun using it, they have seen increases in sales as high as 18 percent from their commissioned salespeople in as few as 30 days.

> When sales managers have learned the importance of reinforcement and begun using it, they have seen increases in sales as high as 18 percent from their commissioned salespeople in as few as 30 days.

The Seven Principles of Positive Reinforcement

Effective reinforcement boils down to seven simple principles. The very best sales managers know that to boost sales, you need to do seven things:

1. Make your reinforcement immediate.

2. Reinforce improvement, not just excellence.

3. Be specific when reinforcing someone.

4. Reinforce new behaviors continuously and good habits intermittently.

5. Capitalize on the Ripple Effect.

6. Know when to reinforce behavior and when to reinforce results.

7. Keep a positive-to-negative feedback ratio of at least 3:1.

Make Your Reinforcement Immediate

To be most effective, reinforcement should follow performance as soon as possible. The more immediate it is, the more powerful it is at turning a behavior into a habit.

Too often, positive feedback is given a day, a week, a month, or even six months after the behavior. When this happens, it doesn't have much effect. It might make you feel good to give it, and it might make the recipient feel good to receive it, but it doesn't do much to get him to continue that behavior. This is why annual performance reviews seldom have any lasting impact.

It is most effective to give reinforcement face-to-face—but that's not always possible, and it's better to give it straightaway over the phone or by voice mail or e-mail than to wait. Let's say your rep Andrea lands a profitable new account on Tuesday but she's on the road and you won't be seeing her for four weeks. Well, it doesn't do much good to wait four weeks to praise her achievement. Call her on Tuesday or Wednesday, when the deal is still fresh in both your mind and hers, to say how pleased you are.

Reinforce Improvement, Not Just Excellence

Almost all sales managers make a big deal if a rep lands a new account that will be worth $1 million each quarter, or they let a rep know they are pleased when he exceeds his month's goal by $32,000 in sales. But they don't say much, if anything, to the guy who's making progress but still isn't quite achieving the results they want. To most of us, praising someone who hasn't yet achieved excellence just doesn't come naturally. But your goal here is to replace reps' bad habits with good habits that are likely to increase sales. That means it is especially important for you to reinforce improvement *as well as* excellence.

> Your goal is to replace reps' bad habits with good habits that are likely to increase sales. That means it is especially important for you to reinforce improvement *as well as* excellence.

Most of us need or appreciate a pat on the back, at least once in a while. People who are making an effort to do things better deserve all the encouragement you can give them.

Take notice of the things a rep is doing right—even if his results aren't as good as you want them to be—and reinforce those behaviors as they occur. You might say, "Looks like you're putting in extra effort finding out *exactly* what the customer wants. That's terrific, because even if it doesn't make a difference to your numbers this week, I know it will pay off in the end."

The rep makes a connection between the behavior and the impact it will have on his results. He now associates identifying customer needs with a positive event: your reinforcement. By praising his behavior, you are helping him form a good habit.

One of the fastest ways to boost sales is to focus your feedback not on the achievement of a particular *level* of sales but on *improvements* in sales or sales-related behaviors. Every time you notice an improvement, tell the person you appreciate the effort. As soon as his performance rises, even from the merely acceptable to just above acceptable, reinforce him—for the improvement he's made, not his current level of performance.

Say you and your rep Mike have agreed to a goal of increasing his unit volume from an acceptable level of 80 to a good level of 100 over the next six months, and he achieves a small boost, from 80 to 83. Although it's tempting to say nothing or to say something like "That's a good start, but you're not there yet," neither of those responses are going to get you where you want to go as fast as you want to get there.

You would be better off saying something like "Mike, I notice your sales have gone from 80 to 83. I really appreciate the effort behind the improvement. You're making good progress toward our intermediate target of 90 by the end of this quarter and then to 100 by the end of the next quarter."

Of course, there's no way you can tell someone who's gone from poor to marginal sales that he's doing a good job. In fact, there are three reasons that's not a good idea:

1. It would be perceived as insincere—because that's what it is—and would have no effect.

2. Mike might reasonably conclude that 83 is "good."

3. It might well cause problems at performance or salary review time.

It is possible, however, to tell him sincerely that he's done a good job of improving, that you appreciate the effort that went into achieving the improvement, that he's making good progress, that you noticed his increased focus, or some other positive aspect of his performance.

If you reinforce improvement, you'll get more improvement—and you'll start to see lasting results within 24 hours.

Make a point of reinforcing people who are striving for or actually making progress, however slight that progress might seem. It's simple: If you reinforce a certain level of performance, you'll get more of that level. If you reinforce improvement, you'll get more improvement—and you'll start to see lasting results within 24 hours.

Be Specific When Reinforcing Someone

Suppose you're sitting face-to-face with Christine, a rep who's just prepared a PowerPoint presentation for a meeting she's got coming up with a potential customer. The presentation has good points but also some areas that need improvement.

The tendency for most sales managers in this situation is to mention what's good in general terms and be more specific about the faults. As in: "Overall, you did a good job on the presentation, Christine, but the first slide is really cluttered, and there aren't enough graphics on any of the slides. Oh yeah, one other thing—you need to work on your punctuation."

This approach doesn't provide enough informational feedback, so Christine will be left feeling uncertain about how to improve the presentation, and it sends negative feedback, even though it started with a compliment.

If you use vague reinforcement like this regularly, it will condition Christine to wait for the other shoe to drop. After being told, "It's good, but . . ." too many times, she will stop hearing the positives and just brace herself for whatever comes after the "but." Eventually, because she fears and expects the criticism, she will become unresponsive to compliments and immune to reinforcement.

Christine and all her fellow reps will begin to assume that every interaction with you will be unpleasant. They'll avoid you or tune you out—maybe both— and you can't help your sales reps improve their performance and boost sales if you can't interact with them!

> Be just as specific about what's right with a person's work as what's wrong with it.

Although they will learn quickly what's wrong about their work, they will never find out what's right with it. For instance, because Christine doesn't know what's right with her PowerPoint presentation, she has no model to follow, so she has nothing to emulate the next time she needs to put together a presentation. She will never become self-sufficient but will always depend on others for guidance.

Be just as specific about what's right with a person's work as what's wrong with it. You might say: "Overall, you did a good job on the presentation, Christine. Now let's review it slide by slide." If it's not a good job overall, you can start with "You've got some good parts here, and you've got some parts that aren't so good. Let's go through everything and see what works and what doesn't.

"The first slide has a lot of text on it, which might make it hard for the customer to read. You handled the next few slides very well. I like the way you summarize the benefits of the Flambole so clearly in bullet points. Double-check slides two through four; they have a couple of punctuation errors, and I made a couple of notes. An additional graph as a summary slide comparing the features and benefits of our new product with our closest competitors' would help the customer understand why ours is a better choice. Slides nine and ten are especially good at explaining why they should switch. I particularly like the way you so clearly demonstrate how the primary features of our valve produce benefits that far outweigh anything our competitors have to offer. Very persuasive."

Review a rep's work in its natural order, rather than puzzling over whether to talk about all the good aspects first and then the bad, or bad then good, or alternating between good and bad. If you put a lot of energy into deciding which aspect to discuss first, the person will get so preoccupied with trying to figure out why you chose that order that she may miss the important feedback you are giving. If you're talking about a pattern of behavior rather than a document, the beginning-to-end rule still applies; you review how the events unfolded, from start to finish.

Reinforce New Behaviors Continuously, Good Habits Intermittently

At first, motivating sales reps to change the way they do their job requires continuous, or almost continuous, positive feedback from you. This means reinforcing virtually everything they do right or every step they take in the right direction. For your sales reps to leave behind old behavior patterns they

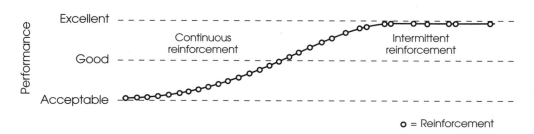

Continuous and intermittent reinforcement

are familiar and comfortable with and adopt new, better ones, they need that continuous support and reinforcement from you. As you can see in the figure, changing their behavior requires a lot of reinforcement.

However, once they reach a good, solid level of performance, you can ease off and switch to intermittent reinforcement, which is less frequent and more random, like the payoff from a slot machine. This works because the habit has now been developed.

Intermittent reinforcement not only saves you the time and effort of reinforcing every single thing a rep does right, it's also more effective. If you keep on continuously reinforcing someone even after she's reached a good performance level, that reinforcement can become almost like a punishment. Suppose you love chocolate milkshakes and are treated to one every single time you do something right; pretty soon, you may actually come to hate chocolate milkshakes. But if you're rewarded for your good behavior at random times—maybe two this week, one the next, and three the following week—you will stay motivated, because you're never quite sure when the payoff is going to come.

If you don't believe intermittent reinforcement works, go watch someone playing a slot machine. He doesn't know *when* it's going to pay off; he just unconsciously knows that if he plays long enough, it *will* pay off.

The question is not, Do you reinforce or not reinforce? The question is, Do you use continuous reinforcement, or do you use intermittent reinforcement? Answer: You use continuous reinforcement to change behavior and intermittent reinforcement to maintain behavior.

One of the reasons intermittent reinforcement works at maintaining behavior is that by the time a sales rep has established the kinds of habits that deliver solid, sustainable results, reinforcement flows from the job itself. For instance, a skilled sales rep knows when he walks out of the sales call whether he's done a good job. He can usually critique the positives and negatives of his own performance, and if he did well, say to himself "Nice job." He has a sense of accomplishment, pride in his work, and a feeling of a job well done. These are *naturally*

> The question is not, Do you reinforce or not reinforce? The question is, Do you use continuous reinforcement, or do you use intermittent reinforcement? Answer: You use continuous reinforcement to change behavior and intermittent reinforcement to maintain behavior.

occurring reinforcers. When a sales rep is getting enough naturally occurring reinforcers, all he needs from you is intermittent affirmation of his value to the company, and some special attention when he's done a really outstanding job.

Unfortunately, such reinforcers are sometimes difficult to come by, especially when a rep is learning a new skill or is new to the job. As managers, we have to supply extra reinforcement until he gets up to speed. For salespeople, naturally occurring reinforcers often grow scarce during slumps in the economy. In turbulent times, even the highest achievers on your team may see a drop in sales and so receive less of the natural reinforcement that comes with a job well done. That's when you have to provide a little extra reinforcement to help keep them motivated in a difficult economic situation.

> In turbulent times, even the highest achievers on your team may see a drop in sales and so receive less of the natural reinforcement that comes with a job well done. That's when you have to provide a little extra reinforcement.

You should also bolster the power of any naturally occurring reinforcers that your reps are getting. In the following three examples, I'll show you how.

Situation 1: A customer e-mails you to let you know that one of your sales reps has gone out of his way in working with her lab to get the new equipment set up and on stream quickly. It's the first you knew anything about it.

You say: Eli, I just got an e-mail from Ellen over at Morris Labs telling me what a great job you did of making sure their equipment was up and running in what she called a "very, very short time frame."

If Eli responds: Well, things did seem to come together pretty well, but helping customers is just part of my job. Besides, Doug over in Tech Support helped a lot, too.

You can say: Well, you're right, it is part of your job. But I still appreciate that kind of effort on your part, because it exemplifies the "above and beyond" part of our corporate values. (Then you should probably also let Doug's boss, Daryn, know about his extra effort.)

Situation 2: Marketing Communications comments on a rep who has made some creative suggestions in the last few months.

You say: Cody, Jackie over in Marketing Communications observed that you've made some great suggestions over the past few months. Two things: First, I appreciate that kind of teamwork with them, because their support is important to us. Second, it must be gratifying to see them take your ideas and come up with something that's going to help us all.

If Cody responds: Well, yes, I guess it does feel pretty good.

You can say: It should, because that kind of outreach and communication is the mark of a real pro.

Situation 3: Someone does a particularly good job but doesn't mention it.

You say: Avis, I just found out that you organized that Murphy job so that we met our original completion date in spite of our earlier setbacks. I also know you kept your extraordinary efforts quiet. I just wanted you to know that your above-and-beyond effort is appreciated.

If Avis responds: Well, I just try to do my job the best I can.

You can say: You sure do. And you do a lot of it on your own. That kind of independent action is the mark of a real professional.

Capitalize on the Ripple Effect

Another real advantage of reinforcement is its rippling-pond effect. When you reinforce one behavior, it increases the frequency of other behaviors of the same type. This means that you can identify a particular desired behavior occuring in a variety of areas of a rep's job and increase the frequency of that behavior in all those areas with relatively little reinforcement.

Joan, for example, was a district sales manager whose reps were responsible for submitting five different types of monthly reports. The reports from Dave were frequently late and incomplete. One day, Joan received a report from Dave that was exactly what she was looking for. It was concise, well written, and to the point; it had a beginning, a middle, and a conclusion; it had a summary paragraph at the end of each section; and it was on time. Pleasantly surprised, Joan immediately told Dave, "I just wanted to take a minute to thank you for the really outstanding job you did on the monthly report. It was concise, well written, and to-the-point; you included a summary paragraph at the end of each section; and you submitted it on time. That's the kind of report that really makes our lives easier around here, and I appreciate the effort I know you must have put into it."

Now, what Joan reinforced was just one behavior in a whole class of behaviors. She reinforced the submission of one report and, specifically, she reinforced those things about the report that were good and that should have been common to all reports. The effect was just like dropping a stone in the middle of a pond: a ripple moves out and affects the entire pond. Joan continued to reinforce Dave, who continued to submit superior reports right on schedule. The reinforcement of the first good report spurred Dave on to do a good job on a particular part of another report, which Joan likewise reinforced. The following month, three out of his five reports were on time, and they were all of a much higher quality.

"So what?" you say. "Why didn't Joan just tell Dave to turn in the report?" As a matter of fact, she had—several times. What would happen, however, is that, after she spoke to Dave, the reports would improve for a while, but their quality would then decline. Then she would speak to him again, and the reports would improve, but only temporarily. Dave had developed what I call a roller-coaster performance pattern.

The roller-coaster pattern is not uncommon—and it's easy to identify and correct. Let's say that we have three possible levels of performance—acceptable, good, and excellent—as shown in the figure. Now, let's imagine that somebody's sales are coasting along at "good" (A) when he suddenly drops to "acceptable" (B). At this point, the sales manager calls him in for a heart-to-heart discussion about why his performance has dropped and how to get him back on track. As a result of this discussion, the rep's performance usually improves, back up to point C. The manager typically responds by saying and doing nothing. After all, although the rep's performance is now good, it's not excellent. But because the rep's efforts go unnoticed, he slacks off again, and his sales drop back down (D). The manager calls him in for another heart-to-heart—and the roller-coaster ride begins again.

The rep receives negative attention when his performance bottoms out but no attention when he improves. And that's just like having no one laugh

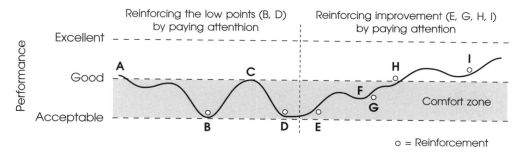

Roller coaster performance, and how to correct it

at your jokes at a party. Some attention, even if it's bad, is better than no attention at all. Fortunately, there is a simple breakout technique. All you need to do is apply the Second Principle of Positive Reinforcement: *Reinforce any improvement, not just excellence.*

This works, too, for pushing reps out of their comfort zone to a higher level of performance. No reps have a completely constant performance level; their efforts often come in bursts, rising and falling within a "comfort zone," and their numbers usually reflect that by rising and falling within a certain range. Wait until a rep's performance rises slightly, and then give him reinforcement (E). His performance will probably continue to improve, and then perhaps he will slack off a bit (F). Ignore or make little of this slacking off—that is, use extinction, or lack of

> I've known countless managers who've used this combination of reinforcement and extinction at the right times to move a sales rep from her comfort zone up to a higher level.

feedback, to extinguish the behavior of slacking off. Then, whenever the rep's effort surges again, reinforce it (G, H, I). I've known countless managers who've used this combination of reinforcement and extinction at the right times to move a sales rep from his comfort zone up to a higher level. Within a very few months, the new zone becomes both comfortable and more productive.

Know When to Reinforce Behavior and When to Reinforce Results

There are two primary things we can reinforce: behavior and results. Results are things such as dollar volume, unit volume, gross margin, customer satisfaction, market share, and any other sales metrics you use in your business; behaviors are the actions your reps take to accomplish those results. As a reminder, here are some behaviors that lead to improved sales results:

- Planning sales calls

- Calling on the right customers

- Identifying customers' needs

As you can see, there's a choice. You can reinforce behavior, you can reinforce sales results, or you can reinforce both. Ideally, you should reinforce both but emphasize either results or behavior, depending upon the particular situation.

Reinforce behavior when:

1. The rep is new to the job or is learning a new skill.

Example: A new rep has asked the right kinds of questions and has done the right kinds of things during a sales call.

Reinforcement: "Bill, I like the way you handled that call. You related well to the buyer, you helped him identify his needs, and you used good questioning techniques. Even though he didn't buy, you obviously know what kinds of things will eventually pay off on the bottom line."

2. Turbulent times prevent the rep from obtaining good results even though he is doing all the right things.

Example: A sales rep is making the right calls and saying the right things, but the economy is adversely affecting sales results.

Reinforcement: "Carl, I noticed that your call frequency is up and that you're contacting our high-potential accounts, but overall sales are still flat. I know that it's sometimes difficult to stay motivated in the face of tough economic times, but you're doing the things we know are critical. Keep up the good work. As soon as the economy starts to turn, you'll see the benefits of all the spade work you're doing now."

3. There is a long time lag between the behavior and the results.

Example: A sales rep is doing and saying the right things in calling on a high-potential account that is difficult to crack.

Reinforcement: "Roger, I know you haven't opened that Flipper Instrument account yet, but the tenacity and persistence you're showing will pay off, not only on that account but on others as well."

In each of these situations, a specific behavior or set of behaviors is reinforced. This, of course, increases the probability that these behaviors will continue, even though the individuals haven't yet experienced the satisfaction of seeing their task completed or accomplished.

Reinforce results when:

1. Everything is running smoothly.

Example: Someone on the inside order desk is keeping average line items per order at a high level.

Reinforcement: "Kate, I don't know how you do it. Our chart shows you still average 10 or more line items per order. That's just super."

2. Results have improved.

Example: Sales have improved slightly but steadily over the last few months.

Reinforcement: "Megan, your district has improved every month for the last four months. Keep doing whatever you're doing, because it's really working well."

3. You want someone to make a mental connection between something he did and the results achieved.

Example: A sales rep does a particularly good job of identifying a customer's needs. When the customer places an order, he shoots you an e-mail to let you know it's because the sales rep was so good at identifying the customer's needs.

Reinforcement: "Ryan, Scott over at Kazoo Products just placed an order for three dozen of our long-eared flamzels. He said the main reason was because you'd done such a good job of helping him identify his needs. Nice going!"

In each of these situations, the rep had done the right things (engaged in the right behavior) and obtained the desired results, so the emphasis of reinforcement was placed on those results. Chances are that the recipient of the reinforcement will continue to practice those behaviors that led to the positive results.

Keep a Positive-to-Negative Feedback Ratio of at Least 3:1

You probably think that you do a pretty good job of delivering positive reinforcement. Chances are that's a pretty good estimate. You probably do a pretty good job.

But pretty good isn't good enough—particularly in tough economic times. We've found that to get the best performance from reps and boost sales you need to maintain at least a 3:1 positive-to-negative feedback ratio. That is, for every piece of negative feedback you deliver, you need to provide at least three pieces of positive feedback—4:1 or 5:1 is even better.

> It's not until a 3:1 positive-to-negative ratio is reached that the rep perceives the relationship as an overall positive.

If your overall feedback ratio for a rep is one piece of negative feedback to one piece of positive feedback, she perceives the overall relationship as mostly negative. If she receives a ratio of two positive pieces to one negative piece of feedback, she see it as neutral. It's not until a 3:1 positive-to-negative ratio is reached that the rep perceives the relationship as an overall positive.

If your ratio is 1:1 and someone asks the rep what it's like to work for you, her response, if she's being polite, would be something like "I'd much prefer to work for someone else."

If it's 2:1, she might say, "Pat's no worse and no better than any other sales manager I've worked for."

At 3:1, her response would be "Pat is great. One of the best sales managers I've ever worked for."

Interested in what your ratio is right now? Here's an easy way to find out. Take a 3 × 5 card. On one side put a plus sign (+); on the other, a minus (−). Every time you deliver positive feedback, put a check mark on the positive side, and every time you deliver negative feedback put a check mark on the negative side. Do it for several days. Then you'll know where your baseline is.

To change it for the better, just put 10 dimes in a pocket at the beginning of each day. Every time you deliver positive feedback to someone, move a dime to the opposite pocket. We know from experience that if you're delivering positive feedback 10 times a day, your positive-to-negative feedback ratio is at least 3:1. If you prefer, keep track on a 3 × 5 card. Do it for 30 days. By then, you should be at a 3:1, 4:1, or 5:1 positive-to-negative feedback ratio. The more uncertain the times, the more important it is to be at 4:1 or 5:1. But make sure you maintain an average of at least 3:1 all the time.

Reinforcement is crucial to motivating your team to reach their goals. So when team members are not yet meeting your expectations, reinforce them continually for everything they do right and for every improvement they make, however small. Once they're performing well, back off and let momentum do the work—but surprise them with reinforcement every now and then. Make it timely, specific, and targeted to the individual, and make it sincere.

Optimize naturally occurring reinforcers—the successes that give your rep a sense of achievement—by adding your own reinforcement. Capitalize on the Ripple Effect by praising the right behavior in one aspect of a rep's job to lead to improvement in similar job behaviors. Get reps out of a roller-coaster pattern of up-down performance by praising improvement and paying little attention to a temporary slacking off.

Focus your reinforcement on reps' behavior when they are learning new skills, sales are down for reasons outside their control, or they have a long period of legwork to do before they can see results. Switch your focus to reinforcing results when a rep shows improvement, consistently gets good results, or you want to emphasize the link between his behavior and a positive result.

For every piece of negative feedback you give, be sure to give the same rep at least three pieces of positive feedback.

Use these basic principles of motivational feedback, along with the informational and developmental feedback we're going to look at in the next two chapters, and you'll be sure to see a whole new level of performance from each and every rep.

6

Informational Feedback: Use Sales Data to Motivate Your Team

NUMBERS ARE THE UNIVERSAL LANGUAGE OF SALES, and chances are that in your company there is no shortage of data. Many sales managers feel confident that the one thing their sales reps do not lack is informational feedback, because they already have access to monthly, weekly, or daily reports on a range of sales metrics.

But not all reports are created equal. The way that informational feedback is selected, focused, and presented can mean the difference between reports that leave salespeople feeling defeated or down, that end up getting glanced at and then forgotten—or that motivate them and help them track their progress.

You and your reps should be able to access data on all the metrics that matter—whether those are dollar and unit volumes, gross margins, new accounts, account penetration, customer satisfaction and retention, market share, growth rate, closing ratio, or any other metric. This information is a valuable—and in too many cases not fully tapped—resource. Exposed to a continuous stream of figures, you can easily overlook its true worth, but if you fully capitalize on it, you can turn raw data into a powerful tool for motivating your team in any kind of economy.

The very best sales managers know that information about performance can boost sales—if it is used as part of an overall performance feedback system. They know that they get results when the information they give their sales teams is

1. goal related

2. relevant

3. measured positively

4. immediate

5. graphic

Focus Feedback on the Goal

A goal is a powerful motivator. Virtually all human behavior is goal directed. That's why making informational feedback relate to the goals your salespeople are striving for gives them a way of identifying which behavior leads them toward accomplishing their goals, and then they know to repeat that behavior. For instance, if your rep sees that doing a better job of identifying profitable potential customers increases her gross margin by 1.5 percent in just one month, that new behavior will become her work habit.

To see how this principle actually works, let's look at one organization that was having problems with its sales—and, as it turned out, with its informational feedback. The company was running at 80 percent of its annual sales target. There was information in its system about how salespeople were performing on a monthly, weekly, and even daily basis—but it wasn't being used, because it wasn't easy to access and wasn't organized in a way an individual rep would find meaningful without going through a number of contortions and calculations. Some reps were receiving quarterly progress reviews, but most were getting only annual performance reviews. Although monthly discussions were held occasionally, nothing was happening on a daily or weekly basis.

> Make informational feedback relate to the goals your salespeople are striving for, because it helps them identify which behavior leads to accomplishing their goals.

To improve sales, the goal-setting cycle was shortened to once a month for all reps who were performing adequately, weekly for those who were performing below expectations, and daily for those who were considerably below par. The IT department set it up so that all reps could quickly see exactly how they were doing each day, as well as how their district, region, and the company were performing. Every time a rep showed improvement or hit his target, he was reinforced with praise. Within six months, the company had shot up from 80 percent of its sales target to more than 130 percent.

Was that due to just the change in informational feedback? No—but that change was the catalyst for other changes, because it gave the sales managers the opportunity to deliver more reinforcement than they had before.

The goal should be built into the reporting system—preferably in a graph—so that sales reps can see, at any time, how they're doing in terms of that goal. To see the benefits of this policy in action, we can look at another company's success story.

Back in chapter 3 we discussed a company that had set a goal to increase sales by a significant amount, and had accomplished that goal—but only because the sales reps simply sold more of the easiest product to sell, the one with the lowest margin. Sales went up, but profitability went down. When that happened, the sales manager made some changes. He established a weekly gross-profit goal for each sales rep and began providing reps each week with an updated graph showing their performance relative to that goal. Within a month, profits were back where they had been, and within two years, profits had doubled. Sales reps had truly become account managers, because they were managing the profitability of their accounts rather than the sales volume of their accounts.

This example also dramatically illustrates why feedback needs to relate not just to a goal but to the correct goal. Indeed, every aspect of your feedback system should be directed toward the correct goal. This means that your informational feedback should align with your reps' goals and the motivational feedback you're giving them.

Everything needs to be aligned. What too often happens is that top managers say they want one thing but really mean that they want something slightly

> The goal should be built into the reporting system—preferably in a graph—so that sales reps can see, at any time, how they're doing in terms of that goal.

different; reps get measured and receive informational feedback on a metric that leads in a slightly different direction, and get paid based on yet another, slightly different metric (maybe different from the one you're paid on); and you're left in the middle trying to decide whether or not you're going crazy.

Give Relevant Information

The informational feedback you give should measure a variable that is relevant to the sales rep receiving it—that is, it should relate directly to her own performance. Occasional updates on how the company is tracking overall are helpful, but the kind of feedback that results in improvement is information that is specific and relevant to the individual and that she has the power to change by altering the way she does her job—such as regular updates on dollar or unit volume, gross margins, new accounts, customer satisfaction, and the like.

If, in addition, you want reps to see more clearly how what they're doing ties into where the company is headed, take a couple of metrics such as gross profit margin and dollar volume and link them into EPS and stock price. As an example, plug in the reps' metrics at the far left of an Excel spreadsheet and plug in EPS and stock price at the far right. Put the associated metrics between those two in their proper sequence on the Excel spreadsheet. Add in the right formulas. Then you can change the gross profit margin and dollar volume numbers, and the resulting impact on EPS and stock price will show up on the far right. It doesn't work miracles, but it does give reps a solid sense of the bigger picture and a clear line of sight between their actions and the impact of those actions on EPS and stock price—and only good can come from that.

Accentuate the Positive

Although it's clear that people react more positively to positive metrics than to negative metrics—accounts won rather than accounts lost, computer uptime rather than computer downtime for IT, home runs rather than strikeouts for baseball players—one of the challenges facing sales is that there seem to be a lot more nos than yeses, and that can be discouraging.

But it doesn't have to be that way.

At the core, there are six categories of responses a customer can give upon being asked for the order:

- "No."

- "I'll listen to what you have to say."

- "I'll consider your product next time for future purchases."

- "I'll recommend your product to Purchasing and my colleagues."

- "I'll specify your product the next time I initiate a purchase order."

- "I'll buy it."

The actual words will vary, but those are the core responses. Most sales managers and most reps look at those and unconsciously see one positive response ("I'll buy") and five variations of "No."

But if you reframe those responses, you can reverse that ratio.

Look at "No" as no—at least until the next conversation. But consider "I'll listen," "I'll consider," "I'll recommend," "I'll specify," and "I'll buy" as variations of yes. Then what you end up with are five various degrees of "Yes" and one version of "No."

This approach is particularly useful when a salesperson has to call on a customer for two, four, six, or even eight months before he gets an order. If these are the kind of sales cycles you're dealing with, I suggest you redesign the metrics you use for giving informational feedback.

First, encourage your salespeople to begin thinking about sales calls as a behavior change program: what the salesperson is really trying to do is change the customer's buying behavior. While the end game is to get the customer to buy from him rather than from someone else, the sales rep actually gets there faster if he focuses on moving the customer from one response to the next—such as from "I'll consider" to "I'll recommend."

> Think of sales calls as a behavior change program: what the salesperson is really trying to do is change the customer's buying behavior.

The rep is then focused less on his presentation and more on what the customer is saying and doing. Although it's a relatively small shift in the rep's behavior, the impact is huge because the rep is focused on the customer—which is exactly where the focus should be.

Then, when a customer moves from "I'll consider" to "I'll recommend," the rep no longer has to walk out of a sales call muttering, "Well, I didn't close that deal" and then turn to pumping himself up for the next call. Instead, he walks out saying, "I'm making progress there, and I'm going to nail this next one." The pumping up still goes on, but it starts from a stronger base and thus has a higher end point.

We've found in our workshops that the fastest way to put this to work is for you to take that list of six customer responses, convert them into what the comparable responses would be from your customers (which may or may not end up being a list of six), and put them into a matrix like this, with potential customers listed across the top:

Potential Key Accounts

Customer Response Stage	A	B	C	D	E
1. "No"	X	X	X	X	X
2. "I'll listen"		X	X	X	X
3. "I'll consider"		X			
4. "I'll recommend"					
5. "I'll specify"					
6. "I'll buy"					

With a simple visual aid like this, you and the sales rep can together establish clear-cut call objectives that are based on typical customer behavior. At the beginning of the week, you might sit down with him and define the call objectives for the week. The sales rep's objective for Customer A would be "to get the customer to listen to me." For B, it would be "to move the customer from 'I'll consider it' to 'I'll recommend it.'" For C, D, and E, the objective would be "to move the customer from 'I'll listen' to 'I'll consider.'"

A system like this serves as a sort of "football field" upon which the sales rep can run. It gives you an opportunity to applaud—reinforce—the rep when he gets the "first down" or even gains a few yards. This avoids the problem that arises with many other feedback systems where there is too much lag time between the initial sales call and the opportunity to give the sales rep reinforcement when he gets the sale. Without a system like this for measuring the extent of customers' behavior change, a rep can get discouraged and ultimately feel resigned to not making particular sales.

You'll also find that the rep's descriptions about where the customer's head is in terms of buying from your firm become clearer and more realistic, thus avoiding the vaguely overoptimistic descriptions that you sometimes hear.

The virtually unseen but very powerful effect is that the rep's feedback positive-to-negative ratio of naturally occurring reinforcers has just gone from 1:5 to just the reverse—5:1. Try it and see. I think you'll be pleased with the results, because when reps are tracking the progress themselves, they have much more ownership of the progress and process—and when they have more ownership, their sales results are better.

People react more positively to positive metrics than to negative metrics.

Measuring performance in positive terms and then reinforcing improved behavior can turn the tide in the right direction. Consider Suzie: she was in most respects a good rep, but when she didn't win the customer immediately, she would too easily become disheartened and move on to other prospects. By not following up, she missed out on opportunities to turn a maybe into a yes. Her manager had emphasized this in the reports he gave her each week—but when he changed the feedback system to track her progress using the grid, she suddenly became more fully engaged in her job. Within seven weeks she was consistently making appropriate follow-ups and her numbers had surpassed the team's average.

Changing to a more positive metric frees reps to think more about problem solving than the problem itself.

Changing the metric also often changes the focal point of a discussion and frees reps to think more about problem solving than the problems themselves. Instead of fretting about why a customer hasn't purchased anything yet, they're thinking about how to move the customer one step closer to yes.

A final note on staying positive when designing your feedback system: informational feedback should never be used as the basis for punishing a sales rep. If a sales manager says, "I don't ever want to catch you with more than 5 percent in that expense category," she probably won't ever catch a rep with more than 5 percent in that expense category. It might happen—she just won't catch anyone. When the feedback system is used as a basis for punishment, people quickly learn that it doesn't pay to tell the truth.

Provide Informational Feedback Immediately

Just as with reinforcement, informational feedback should be immediate. The sooner your reps get feedback about their performance, the better able they are to relate specific job behaviors to specific results. For instance, they are more likely to relate new behavior such as sales call planning, identifying customers' needs, or increasing the number of times they ask for the sale during a call with an increase in new accounts, gross margin, or unit volume.

The more quickly you give your reps feedback, the sooner they can gauge whether their behavior is working or whether they need to change the way they are doing their job. Therefore, you should shorten the feedback cycle wherever you can. Depending upon your type of sales, even hourly feedback may be appropriate—for instance, on an inside order desk, where sales occur continually throughout the day.

> The more quickly you give your reps feedback, the sooner they can gauge whether their behavior is working or whether they need to change the way they are doing their job.

I've found that as reps receive more immediate feedback on how they're doing, they begin to act as their own supervisors. Though it might seem that giving immediate feedback would be a time drain, sales managers who implement this principle find that in fact their job takes less energy and they're able to accomplish more, because their reps are better equipped to self-motivate and correct their behavior when they need to.

In one situation I encountered, three reps at the inside order desk weren't asking for additional business. Sure, they were taking the orders, but they weren't suggesting related items or regularly mentioning the daily or weekly specials. Once a month, the branch manager would sit them down, show them the figures for average number of line items per order, and ask them to try to do better the next month. For a brief period, they seemed to try a bit harder to get additional business over the phone, but the branch manager made no attempt to measure this improvement immediately and update them on their progress, and they would again stop suggesting additional items and asking for that business.

Then the branch manager decided to change the feedback system. Every day he would post a graph, which he worked with IT to create, showing the average number of line items per order for all three salespeople combined and an individual graph for each salesperson. Almost immediately, the average number of line items per order climbed from 5 to 9.3. Thanks to the shortened feedback cycle, the inside order salespeople are now aggressively and consistently working to maintain that average number of line items per order, and to improve it. Naturally, the branch manager delivered the appropriate amount of reinforcement (lots of it) every time the number of line items per order ticked up.

Make It Simple and Graphic

People don't always "get" numbers, but most understand images right away. Graphics are therefore one of the most important parts of an effective feedback system. What I'm suggesting is that this:

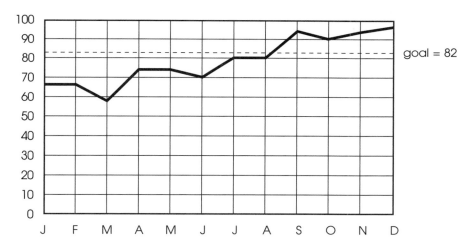

has much more of an impact on your sales reps' behavior and motivation than this:

January	66	July	80
February	66	August	80
March	58	September	94
April	74	October	90
May	74	November	94
June	70	December	96

To be most effective, graphs should be:

Simple. The measurement unit—dollar volume, unit volume, new accounts opened, or gross margins maintained, for example—should be indicated on the left-hand side, on the vertical axis. The time scale over which you are tracking the metric—hours, days, weeks, months—should appear on the bottom, horizontal, axis.

Specific. Focus on one sales metric only on each graph. A lot of managers chart four or five variables on a single graph—using a dotted line for one, a thick line for another, a thin line for a third, and so on—but I've found that most people are better able to understand if you graph one variable at a time. So instead of this:

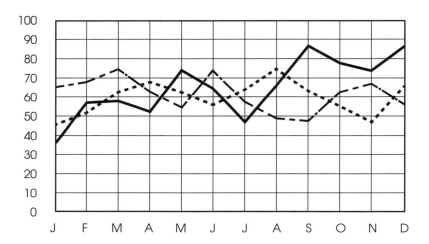

simply make three graphs with a strong solid line on each.

Goal driven. Be sure to include the goal to be reached by the sales reps, and put their actual results in another color so it's easy for them to see where they are now in relation to their goal. In the graph on the next page, the sales rep is tracking around 55 units per month; his ultimate goal is 90, but his manager has asked him to aim above 65 in the next three months.

Line graphs. The most motivating type of graph is a line graph showing your salespeople's progress for that month, week, day, or even hour if appropriate. Cumulative graphs that show sales over a year can be discouraging, because if sales are considerably behind target several months into the year, people see no way of hitting the year-end goal. Bar graphs focus more on an

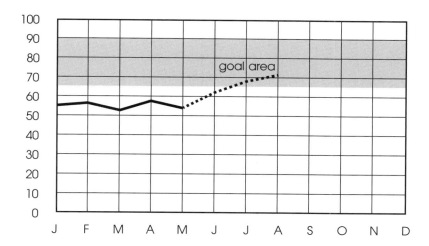

absolute level of sales rather than a change in performance, which should be your focus here.

Competitive. A graph displayed on the wall that charts team performance, combined with individual graphs that are kept private between you and each salesperson, encourage healthy competition: the team tries to beat the team goal, and each individual tries to beat his own record. Avoid displaying a graph comparing individual salespeople; it fosters the wrong kind of competition, individuals against one another. Will reps still talk about their numbers with each other? Of course they will! They're sales reps. But it's their choice to do that, and because it's their choice, they frequently end up coaching one another on what's working and what's not working. That not only saves you time, it saves the pushback that can come from reps when you try to tell them, "Eddie finds that this is working for him."

Information about performance can be a powerful motivator for boosting sales—if that information is used as part of a coherent performance feedback system in which goals, expectations, reinforcement, and informational feedback are all working together to lead your team in the right direction.

Make sure that you (and IT) are delivering your salespeople timely information on key indicators that show whether their sales approach is delivering results. Focus on positive metrics rather than those that are expressed in the negative. Remember to avoid using information for punishment purposes, so your reps don't try to hide the truth from you. Finally, make your informational feedback simple and graphic so it is clear and its meaning has impact.

When you integrate this informational feedback with reinforcement every time your reps show improvement, you will then be fully capitalizing on a resource that is already available to you—your sales metrics—and transforming that information into a potent motivator to boost sales.

CHAPTER

7

Developmental Feedback:
A Positive Approach
to Nonperformance

THERE WILL BE OCCASIONS when, despite all your efforts at applying the principles we've covered so far, an underperforming team member does not make any effort to improve, or makes an effort but still doesn't come close to meeting his target. If a salesperson is consistently falling short of achieving the results you need, it's time to sit down with him face-to-face and address the problem.

No sales manager looks forward to this kind of conversation, because all too often it spirals downward in a familiar negative pattern:

"Ken, we've talked about your unit sales levels before, and still you're averaging only four a week. What do you have to say for yourself?"

"Well, you know, because the economy's so tight and the market's so competitive, customers think they can just get more and more out of us. Now they seem to think we should be able to move mountains for them, and when the mountains don't move, they cut back on ordering."

"But you're a much better salesperson than these figures show. Why aren't we seeing sales results that are as good as you should be capable of?"

"Ever since Modular cut their prices by 12 percent or whatever it was, everything's gone down the drain here."

"But even with their price cut, our prices are still competitive with theirs, so that can't explain the low sales numbers."

So common is this pattern that it may seem almost inevitable that any time you need to confront a sales rep about nonperformance you end up bogged down in irrelevant arguments like this. The discussion gets off on the wrong foot, the sales rep becomes defensive or hostile, and maybe you do, too. You end up getting nowhere—except irritated with each other.

But there is another way.

The very best sales managers get results when they discuss performance issues, because they

1. define the issue factually,

2. ask for solutions using the right questions,

3. explore options,

4. reinforce positive responses, and

5. close the deal.

By following these five steps, you'll be able to discuss performance issues in a way that elicits a commitment to improve, rather than just excuses or grudging compliance.

Preparing to Give Developmental Feedback

I am amazed how often a sales manager who would chew a rep out for "winging it" on a sales call due to inadequate planning might himself simply wing it when he has to bring that same rep in for a discussion about poor performance. For developmental feedback to be effective—for it to actually bring about lasting change in the rep's performance—you need to plan it carefully. In fact, you need to be as thoughtful about this discussion as you were when you first sat down with the rep and set the goals that he is now falling short of achieving.

Before you have this discussion with an underperforming sales rep, first review the previous chapters to make sure that you are demonstrating belief in the rep, that the goals are clear and have action plans where appropriate, that reinforcement—particularly of improvement—has been delivered, and that informational feedback is available.

Then make sure that there is no outside factor blocking the rep from reaching his goal—for instance, a manufacturing or shipping issue, a strike at his largest customer, or something similar.

You may find it helpful to write down what you want to say to the rep, based on the five steps outlined in this chapter. Write down the exact words you will use for the first minute or two, when you're setting the tone. Anticipate reactions and be prepared to address them. The purpose of your notes is not to have a script to follow, but to have firmly embedded in your mind what words and phrases you want to use to move the discussion forward in a positive fashion.

> Write down the exact words you will use for the first minute or two, when you're setting the tone.

Your notes are for your eyes only, not to be brought into the meeting, although some sales managers find it useful to have three or four key words jotted down to keep them on track for the first few minutes. The sales rep should be at ease and not feel that you've already made up your mind about him, so you don't want to look or sound scripted.

You may also find it helpful to role-play the discussion with someone beforehand. Role-playing gives you the chance to fine-tune what you plan to say, in order to steer the discussion toward the most positive result.

Arrange a time to meet with the sales rep, letting him know specifically what it is that you want to discuss. Give the rep time to think about the situation before the discussion, but not so much time that he begins to worry. The best time to schedule the discussion is later the same day; don't let more than three days pass. Let the rep know that this will be a positive conversation about ways to improve, not a chewing-out session.

Before you discuss performance issues with a sales rep:

- Review your own goal-setting and feedback systems.
- Check for obstacles blocking the rep's path.
- Write notes or role-play the discussion.
- Set up a meeting no more than three days away.
- Tell the rep specifically the issue that you want to address.
- Put the sales rep at ease.

For example, if you want to talk with Jason about his failure to return customer calls promptly, tell him that. Say something like, "Jason, we need to discuss our expectation of promptly returning calls to customers. I've noticed that some of the customers in your region report that we're missing our two-hour target. Before the end of the week, I'd like to figure out how we can start hitting that two-hour turnaround consistently. Between now and Friday, when is the best time for you to sit down with me and discuss that?"

As you open the discussion, set a pleasant tone. Put the sales rep at ease, because until he is comfortable, he will be using his energy to cope with the stress of the meeting rather than focusing on performance improvement. Although creating a relaxed atmosphere shouldn't feel artificial or contrived, it can be planned. A brief exchange about how your team did over the weekend or the latest episode of a TV show you both watch will open the discussion and help reduce tension.

1. Define the Issue Factually

Before you ask any questions, state the performance issue. Make it a plain statement of fact. Don't be judgmental, don't blame anybody, and don't jump to evaluating the problem. A sales rep may see a discussion about her performance problems as a personal attack, so if you begin judgmentally you will probably receive in return a defensive response or a counterattack. Nobody wins those battles. Instead, define the performance issue factually, almost like you're giving informational feedback. It's not positive; it's not negative. It just is.

Defining the issue: examples

Avoid	Use
"Carole, we've talked about your unit sales figures before, and here we are again. Why did they slip?"	"Carole, I've noticed that over the last six months your unit sales have sometimes slipped below 80."
"Paul, I'm really disappointed your customers are so dissatisfied with you."	"Paul, I've looked at the customer satisfaction ratings for the past quarter, and I see that you're tracking between 3.8 and 4.3."
"Pam, don't you know how important new accounts are?"	"Pam, I notice that you didn't call on any potential new accounts last month."

Think of your statement as a mirror. If the facts you state are clear and indisputable—not loaded with opinion or blame—the sales rep will see an exact image of her own behavior. Then she can begin to change that behavior.

The rep should understand that you are not attacking her but simply describing a behavior that needs to be addressed and solved. The underlying message should be "I like and respect you, but not your behavior." This way, you avoid putting the rep on the defensive, which makes it easier to get to the heart of the problem in the next step.

> The underlying message should be "I like and respect you, but not your behavior."

2. Ask for Solutions Using the Right Questions

Follow up your statement by asking the rep for ideas on how to solve the problem, using a question that is

- future oriented,

- open-ended, and

- neutral.

Future oriented

Future-oriented questions focus on how you and the rep can improve something from now on, rather than on what went wrong in the past. Historical questions, which focus on what has already happened, should be avoided, because they make the other person defensive and angry, and they don't lead to solutions. The person's usual response is to simply make excuses. You may be familiar with this pattern in conversations you've had with reps:

Manager: "Helen, why did your unit sales figures drop?"

Sales rep: "The truth is, the economy's just really bad and people aren't spending like they used to; and since head office brought in that price increase in May, people are even less likely to buy from us. Plus the online retailers are deep-discounting just to steal our market share."

Manager: "Helen, I'm trying to solve a problem here, but all I'm getting from you is a bunch of excuses."

As a sales manager, you do need to find out why a rep's results are poor, but there are better ways to do it than to ask point-blank for the reason. Questions that look to the past, such as "Why did this happen?" or "Who caused this problem?" ask for reasons but invite excuses. Managers don't like excuses, so they get upset when a rep offers them.

If you ask the wrong question, you'll get the wrong answer—one that doesn't give you the information you need.

The fault in the example above is the manager's as much as the rep's. All she was doing was trying to answer the question "Why?" If you ask the wrong question, you'll get the wrong answer—one that doesn't give you the information you need. What is truly important is rectifying the situation in the future, so ask the sales rep to articulate how the problem can be corrected or her behavior improved. For instance: "Helen, how can we get your unit sales up where they need to be?"

Though this question doesn't ask directly for an explanation of the poor performance, if the rep can articulate how her behavior can be improved, she's already done the brain work necessary to determine what went wrong, and usually she'll explain that at the same time as she's offering her solution. That means you don't even need to press her for an admission of guilt.

Open-ended

You'll notice that as well as being future oriented, "How can we get your unit sales up to where they need to be?" is also an open-ended question—one that requires an active response. If you asked, "Helen, can you increase your unit sales to where they need to be?" you might just get a yes or a no. Then the communication channel would be closed, and you'd have to begin the discussion all over again. Ask an open-ended question and you'll be able to continue the conversation and find a solution to the problem.

Neutral

Your question also needs to be neutral, and that means avoiding questions that begin with why or who. When you ask a sales rep, "Who told you

Asking for solutions: examples

Avoid	*Use*
Historical questions: "Why were sales so low?"	Future-oriented questions: "How can we get sales back over 85 units a month?"
Closed questions (with yes/no answers): "Is it possible to improve market share?"	Open-ended questions (with active responses): "What steps can we take to improve market share?"
Why or who (loaded): "Why are you letting the economy have so much effect on your sales?"	What, when, where, how, which (neutral): "What can we do to counter the effects of the slowdown in the economy?"

to do your sales calls that way?" or "Why did you miss your target?" it sounds as though you're trying to lay blame, and quite naturally, the rep becomes defensive. Neutral questions—beginning with what, when, where, how, or which—rarely trigger a defensive reaction. They keep the discussion more positive and constructive.

Try to include the word "we," because it promotes the idea of a team, and it may encourage your sales rep to let you know if there is something you can do differently to help her get back on track.

3. Explore Options

Once you've asked for solutions, think of the next part of the discussion as a brainstorming session. Your aim now is to get your rep talking about options and alternatives that will get his sales performance back on track. Don't evaluate each solution as it comes up, just write down any suggestions the rep wants to make. Your rep may be feeling stressed and frustrated during

> Get your rep talking about options and alternatives that will get his sales performance back on track.

this meeting, and his ideas may reflect that. That's okay. Just respond as neutrally as possible and get the ideas down on paper. Don't stop as soon as you hear the answer you want to hear, but let the ideas flow.

The difficult part of this for many sales managers is resisting the urge to jump in and explain why a particular idea won't work. If a sales rep comes up with something wacky, you'll probably be tempted to shoot the idea down in flames—but if you stay neutral and keep asking for options and alternatives, there's a good chance your rep will find the solution to the problem:

Manager: "How can we increase sales on a unit volume basis?"

Sales rep: "Drop the price by 20 percent."

Manager: "Okay, one possibility is to reduce the price. How else might we be able to increase sales volume?"

Sales rep: "I think our sales might improve if we had new point-of-purchase advertising. I've been noticing that they get bent out of shape easily."

The less you talk, the more suggestions he will make, and the more he'll feel he owns the solution. With a sense of ownership, he is more likely to work hard to put the idea into effect. So when you write down the rep's ideas, try to stick as closely as possible to his wording, because this increases his feeling of ownership.

> The less you talk, the more suggestions the sales rep will make, and the more he'll feel he owns the solution.

If the rep offers only vague answers or excuses, or tries to blame someone else, try posing further neutral questions, beginning with what or how, to pin him down to specifics and steer the discussion toward future goals. Three examples:

Exploring the Options: Example A

Manager: "How can we get sales back up where they should be?"

Sales rep: "Well, I don't know what we can do. Sales are down everywhere, not just at our company."

Exploring the Options: Example B

Manager: "I've noticed that, too, but how can we counter the effect of dropping sales here?"

Sales rep: "I really don't know. The economy is so tight."

Exploring the Options: Example C

Manager: "Yes, it is tight. What can we do to get a bigger slice of the market?"

Sales rep: "I guess I could make an effort to target some new potential big accounts next month . . . and maybe an even faster way would be to try to get more business each month from two or three of our current accounts who we know are also buying from one of our competitors."

4. Reinforce Positive Responses

Reinforce any useful suggestions that the sales rep makes, either in words or by nodding, smiling, increasing eye contact, or leaning forward. This bolsters the rep's confidence, encourages creativity, and makes it more likely that she will keep coming up with useful ideas on how to improve her performance.

> Reinforce the options that have the most merit—those that have a real possibility of paying off and can realistically be implemented.

Once you feel you've got most of the alternatives out on the table, your aim is to reinforce the options that have the most merit—those that have a real possibility of paying off and can realistically be implemented. How do you know which have solid merit? It's a judgment call, but you'll know:

Reinforcing Positive Responses: Example A

Sales rep: "I think our sales might improve if we had new point-of-purchase advertising. I've been noticing that they get bent out of shape easily."

Manager: "That's an excellent suggestion. That's the kind of thing that's going to improve our sales right where the rubber meets the road."

Reinforcing Positive Responses: Example B

Sales rep: "I could make an effort to target an additional five new potential big accounts next month."

Manager: "I like that sort of enthusiasm and commitment to hard work. That's the kind of thinking that will get your sales back up to where they can and should be."

Reinforcing Positive Responses: Example C

Sales rep: "I could select seven or eight customers this month and look at their purchasing patterns to determine what type of additional products might benefit them."

Manager: "That's smart thinking. There's almost always some additional business to be had, and committing to a target like that is the way to grow our sales."

5. Close the Deal

Once you've identified the most effective ideas from your brainstorming, work toward a commitment from your sales rep to achieve a goal. You need to

- summarize your discussion and propose a goal,

- state positive expectations, and

- follow up.

Summarize Your Discussion and Propose a Goal

Together set a goal that equates to improved performance, and get a commitment from the sales rep to achieve that goal within a certain time frame by adopting the most effective ideas from your discussion.

Closing the Deal: Example A

Manager: "I think we've agreed that we need to bring your gross margin up to a good, solid 22. Which of the steps, or combination of steps, that you've suggested would move you up to 22?"

Sales rep: "I think that by combining the idea of point-of-purchase materials with the one about selecting five or six high-potential accounts where we don't have much penetration, we could reach our target."

Manager: "Those both sound good, Charlie. How long would it take to get you to 22 if we put those in effect right away?"

Sales rep: "I think we could get there in three months."

Manager: "That sounds realistic to me. Let me just see if I can summarize what we've talked about here. . . ."

There may be times when the discussion doesn't go quite as smoothly as this, in which case you may have to be a little more flexible, and ask several more future-oriented, open-ended, and neutral questions before you get a final commitment:

Closing the Deal: Example B

Manager: "I think we've agreed that we need to bring your gross margin up to a good, solid 22. Which of the steps, or combination of steps, that you've suggested would move you up to 22?"

Sales rep: "I can't get to 22."

Manager: "Well, how close do you think you can get?"

Sales rep: "I think I can get to 20."

Manager: "Which of your suggested solutions do you think will get you there the fastest, Charlie?"

Sales rep: "I think that providing the new point-of-purchase materials for the higher-margin products and looking at the five or six high-potential accounts where we don't have much penetration would be best."

Manager: "If we put both of those ideas into effect, Charlie, are you saying that would get us to 20 or 22?"

Sales rep: "Well, for sure that should get us to 20—maybe to 22."

Manager: "What kind of time frame are we looking at?"

Sales rep: "Oh, three or four months. "

Manager (with a smile): "Okay, Charlie, you know what my next question is going to be."

Sales rep (with a bigger smile): "Twenty in three months and
22 in four months."

Manager: "Done deal! Let me know how I can help. "

In the second example, the manager doesn't get quite as enthusiastic a commitment from Charlie. Nonetheless, it's clear that Charlie is involved and feels
committed to solving the problem. If his manager reinforces him when he makes
even a little progress, Charlie will continue to do a better job, and momentum
will build. In the majority of cases, after about the same amount of time, reps
who were eager and reps who were hesitant to commit to a new goal end up with
about the same performance—as long as their improvements are reinforced.

State Positive Expectations

During your wrap-up, include positive expectations about the rep's ability to meet their new goal, as in, "Well, Charlie, I think I agree with you that
the new point-of-purchase materials and targeting those high-potential accounts will get your average back in the 22-point range. You're one of our
most capable sales reps, and you have the skills to do this."

Follow Up

Finally, as part of the agreement, arrange a time to meet again. It is important to get together again to discuss how the rep is progressing. The fact
that his performance was lagging prior
to your discussion is probably a good
indicator that he needs more immediate feedback. Scheduling a follow-up
meeting also reminds the rep that the
issue you've just discussed is serious.

Check the sales rep's progress, and reinforce
any sign of improvement. People are quick
to assume that if no one is checking on
what they are doing, no one cares.

It is important that you keep any
promises you made to take steps to
help the sales rep meet his goal. Your conscientious effort to do what you
promised will help strengthen the sales rep's resolve to do the same.

Be sure to check that the sales rep is meeting milestones on the way to his
goal. People are quick to assume that if no one is checking on what they are doing, no one cares—and no sales rep is going to feel motivated if he thinks you
don't care. Reinforce any sign of improvement. Straight after your discussion

about his nonperformance, he is likely to show an immediate improvement. But this is only a shot in the arm. Without proper follow-up reinforcement, the new behavior will be extinguished and the old behavior will reappear.

When faced with a sales rep's performance issues, first check that you have everything you need in place to enable your reps to succeed and improve: that you are communicating positive expectations, setting goals and action plans, reinforcing good behavior and improvement, and giving the right informational feedback. If a rep is still falling short despite these systems, it is time to supportively confront her nonperformance.

Take the time to prepare and plan for a discussion that addresses the problem in a positive way, focusing on the achievement of future goals.

Whatever you do, don't resort to the "Sandwich Interview." You know these—they go something like this:

Open up with a couple of nice things for the top of the sandwich: "Hey, Josh, come on in. Sit down. How about that game on Saturday? Whaddaya think of the weather?"

Get to the real meat of the discussion: "You know, Josh, you got some real problems in your sales numbers," *followed by much gnashing of teeth and detailed descriptions of Josh's shortcomings.*

Close with a pep talk for the bottom of the sandwich: "Well, Josh, you certainly have the ability and the motivation. Get out there and rock 'em this week."

You can see what's coming a mile away, and so can Josh.

If you do have some good points and some bad points to cover, follow the suggestion from chapter 5: simply cover them in their natural sequence.

Define the performance issue in a factual way that doesn't lay blame, and then ask for solutions. Phrase your questions so that they look to the future and not the past, require an active response rather than just a yes or no, and use neutral words such as how and what rather than why or who.

Let your sales rep's ideas flow without evaluating them. Use reinforcement—nodding, smiling, and positive statements—especially when she suggests useful ideas. Work toward a commitment from your sales rep to achieve a new goal by implementing the options that have the most merit. Make it clear that you have positive expectations of her and confidence that she can achieve her goal. Be sure to follow up with feedback, and arrange another meeting to check in on your rep's progress.

8

Putting It All to Work

NOW THAT YOU'VE LEARNED how the best sales managers motivate their reps to improve performance, it is time for you to put these tools into practice in your own job. You may need to introduce all of the techniques we've looked at—or perhaps you're already using some or even all of these techniques but not as effectively as you could.

In a nutshell, to bring about the most improvement in your sales reps, you need to

- communicate positive expectations,

- establish appropriate goals,

- make action plans for meeting those goals,

- hold reps accountable,

- provide regular informational feedback showing progress,

- reinforce good and improved performance, and

- confront nonperformance in a positive way that leads to a commitment to improve.

The real learning is going to happen over the next few months, because unless you are different from all the other sales managers I have worked with, you'll stub your toe at least once. And every stubbed toe will be a learning situation that will strengthen your skills.

To help you on your way, here are some guidelines for applying these tools in your business and life.

Become a Behavioral Engineer

As we have seen, to boost sales, your aim should be to change the behavior of your sales reps so that they leave behind bad habits and consistently start doing the things that improve sales metrics. So to make the tools in this book effective, you need to stop thinking about your reps in generalized terms like "motivated," "good attitude," or "bad attitude." Specific behaviors, rather than generalizations about attitude and motivation, should be your focus.

Specific behaviors, rather than generalizations about attitude and motivation, should be your focus.

Focus on Changing Reps' Behaviors, Not Attitude or Motivation

Frequently, a sales manager will say something like "Ken, if you're going to make it in this company, you simply have to be more aggressive." Ken will probably nod and say, "Well, I'll put my shoulder to the wheel. I'll get out there and be a little more aggressive." But because the manager hasn't articulated exactly what behavior he wants from Ken, this approach is doomed to failure.

The best sales managers know that they need to identify specific examples of behavior that Ken does, or does not do, that make him not aggressive enough as a salesperson. It turns out that Ken asks for the order only once or twice during a sales call and gives up if the customer doesn't show interest. Now the manager's job is to engineer a change in Ken's behavior by saying, for example:

"On sales calls, I think you do a good job of positioning our company and products to the customer and relating to his needs. But I think you could do a better job in terms of asking for the order. I've kept track, and you average 1.4 times per call. The studies I've seen show you can ask for an order three, four, or five times without seeming pushy, because often the customer doesn't even hear the first couple of times. So, Ken, I'd like for us to work together to get the number of times you ask for the order up to an average of at least two, preferably closer to three."

This focuses on a specific task—increasing the number of times the rep asks for the order each sales call—that will develop the kind of behavior pattern that leads to improved results.

It is common for a sales manager to have a certain number of reps in her team who seem to require more managerial support than most. She may wish that these reps were more motivated and didn't need her to identify opportunities and solve every problem. But what she really means when she says they aren't motivated enough is that they are not performing up to her desired level. If they were, she would say they were "motivated." We can't actually see attitude or motivation, so we draw conclusions based on the behavior we observe.

> Focus on a specific task that will develop the kind of behavior pattern that leads to improved results.

What the best sales managers understand is that the only thing they can really affect is their reps' behavior—for instance, thorough pre-call planning, making cold calls, or carefully identifying all the individuals in an account who will influence the buying decision. By changing the behaviors associated with attitude or motivation, they see improvements in performance.

When it comes to behavioral engineering, the best sales managers

- clarify the results their reps need to achieve,

- identify specific examples of behaviors that impact on specific metrics, and

- look for ways to change those behaviors in their reps.

This means you should focus not on the nonbehaviors shown in the table on the next page, but on changing the behaviors in order to improve the metrics.

Am I suggesting that you never use words like perseverance or persevere? Not at all, because they can be handy as general labels. What I am suggesting is that you don't make those your focal point. Rather than saying to a rep, "Bodie, you need to persevere more," you can simply say, "Bodie, you need to

Nonbehaviors	Behaviors	Metrics (Results of Behavior)
Bad attitude	Making cold calls	Dollar volume
Good attitude	Thanking a customer	Unit volume
Motivation	Identifying customers' needs	Gross margins maintained
Friendliness	Providing swift responses	New accounts opened
Courteousness	Using "feel, felt, found"	Account penetration
Aggressiveness	Detailed call planning	Customer satisfaction
Neatness	Explaining product benefits	Customer retention
Cheerfulness	Submitting reports on time	Market share
Dedication	Anticipating objections	Growth rate
Perseverance	Pre-popping objections	Closing ratio

Nonbehaviors, behaviors, and metrics

persevere more by calling on accounts no less than once a month and staying with a problem a customer has until it's solved"—or whatever behaviors you need Bodie to demonstrate.

Change Your Own Behavior

If you want your reps to change their behavior, you have to change your own behavior first. You have to look at the behavior in your sales reps that you wish to modify. Then you have to examine your own behavior and ask yourself, "What do I have to do—what changes do I have to make in my own behavior—in order to promote behavior change in others?"

> If you want your reps to change their behavior, you have to change your own behavior first.

Problems—such as a sales rep performing below expectations—arise for a multitude of reasons, most of which are not necessarily any one person's fault. But if you are like most sales managers I've worked with, once problems arise, they get locked into your relationships with your reps and take on a life of their own. In trying to deal with those problems, you may find yourself in patterns that lead you around in circles.

What you need is to break out of the cycle by looking toward the future. Change your own behavior by making it a habit to set clear goals with your reps and hold them accountable for those goals. Hold them accountable by reinforcing them when they show improvement and by confronting their nonperformance in a supportive and positive way.

The Three Elements Are Interrelated

We have established the importance of believing in them, holding them accountable, and providing supportive feedback. These three elements can be envisioned as a three-legged stool: if one leg is missing, the stool doesn't function very well. To lead your sales team to better sales, you need to make sure that all three legs are on the stool.

If you believe in your sales reps and hold them accountable but don't give them supportive feedback, you don't have a functioning behavior-change system.

If you hold your reps accountable and give them supportive feedback but have very low expectations of their performance, you don't have a functioning behavior-change system.

The tools in this book will change your reps' behavior and boost your sales only when all three elements are in place and working well together.

It's Okay to Be Tough

We have focused a lot on reinforcement and being positive—but there's nothing wrong with being tough. In fact, it's often appropriate. The tools

Belief, accountability, and feedback are interrelated

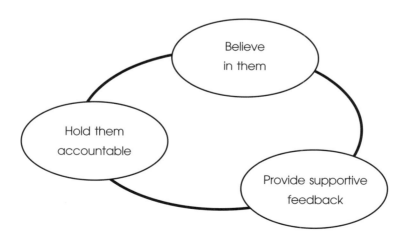

in this book are really about behavior change, which is a tough assignment. Sometimes you have to push people off dead center to get them moving in a new direction.

Set tough goals. Being tough might mean asking or telling a rep that he has to step up production, as in this example:

Sales manager: We are currently averaging sales of 230 units per week in your territory, and without stealing volume from the future, we need to bump that up to somewhere between 270 and 280.

Rep: I'm not sure we can do it.

Sales manager: Well, I'm sure you can. You're smart, you're good at your job, and you've got the skill set to do it. Let's look at what options we have for getting there.

Toughness doesn't mean chewing people out. When we chew a rep out it's usually because we're angry or frustrated and it makes us feel better. But it sure doesn't make the rep feel better, and it almost never produces any change in the rep's behavior except in the very short run. As we've seen in the previous chapters, there are plenty of better ways to get lasting behavior change. And although chewing someone out may temporarily stop them from doing the wrong behavior, it doesn't necessarily get the right behavior to occur. You get the right behavior when you reinforce the right behavior.

> Sometimes you have to push people off dead center to get them moving in a new direction.

If you do chew someone out, do it sparingly, do it quickly, don't overdo it, and be sure to reinforce the right behavior as soon as it occurs. Too often, a sales rep gets chewed out and shows some improvement but doesn't receive reinforcement. So he slides back. Then he gets chewed out again, shows a little burst of improvement, and again receives no reinforcement. If this happens too many times, he'll just give up.

Make These Tools Part of Your Job

After reading this book, you might be saying to yourself, "I think this guy is trying to add an awful lot to my job." But the truth is, I'm really not adding anything to your job; I'm suggesting a better way of doing it. The sales management system I have outlined doesn't work as a program that lasts a month or six months or a year—it's simply a way of doing your job. Think of it as a slightly different way to do many things you are probably already doing.

Remember 5-90-5

Out of every 100 employees, there's a 5-90-5 ratio. Five percent of your reps are top performers—dependable, responsible, cooperative, motivated and motivating. Sales managers sometimes tend to ignore them. After all, they're already top performers, so why bother? The reason you need to remember to apply these tools to them is that by communicating positive expectations and occasionally applauding their efforts, you make sure that they will stay top performers. In fact, you will make them even stronger.

> I'm really not adding anything to your job; I'm suggesting a different way of doing it that will make your reps much more productive.

The middle 90 percent are the ones you really need to target with the tools in this book, because that's where you're going to get the most bang for the buck. That 90 percent can climb up closer to the top 5 percent or slide downward toward the bottom 5 percent. It all depends on you. Because this is the bulk of your sales team, that's where the most "juice" is. Move the bottom 5 percent by 10 percent and you do okay. Move the top 5 percent by 10 percent and you do a little bit better. Move the middle 90 percent by 10 percent and you have just bumped up sales by a ton.

That bottom 5 percent can cause trouble, demotivate, and have a negative effect on your company. Maybe they shouldn't be there, but they are. If you apply the tools in this book when you deal with them, you will probably

> Move the middle 90 percent by 10 percent and you have just bumped up sales by a ton.

be able to change them a bit—but it may not be worth the effort. You have a fiduciary responsibility to the company, and that means you need to invest your time and energy on those areas that bring the highest return to the company and its shareholders.

While I would argue—from a theoretical point of view—that these tools will work on anyone, the time and energy to get them to work on much of that bottom 5 percent simply won't produce a good ROI. My advice is to do what you should have done months ago—take a hard look and decide whether they should stay or go. That decision is one that you have to make dispassionately. If the answer is "go," then you have to carry it out compassionately. Give the person the appropriate support to leave and find a job somewhere else. That allows you to concentrate on the 90 percent—where the real payoff to your efforts lies—while also remembering to acknowledge your top 5 percent.

> Concentrate on the 90 percent—where the real payoff to your efforts lies—while also remembering to acknowledge your top-performing 5 percent.

Integrate These Tools into Your Reward and Recognition Program

All too frequently, reward and recognition programs are ineffective because they are set up in a way that conflicts with the company's goal. For instance, the program may be based on sales, rather than on the company's real goal, profitability.

> All too frequently, reward and recognition programs are ineffective because they are set up in a way that conflicts with the company's goal.

Another common conflict goes like this: The company says, "Customer satisfaction is our most important value." Sounds good. But when you look at incentive trip criteria, customer satisfaction isn't even in the mix. That's one of the reasons you need to integrate what you have just learned about feedback—and in particular, motivational feedback (chapter 5)—into your reward and recognition program.

People are most highly motivated when both their financial and psychological needs are met, so the most effective reinforcement system mixes equal parts reward, which is primarily economic, and recognition, which is primarily psychological—with both being in alignment with your company's strategic intent. The next figure shows a framework our clients find helpful in making sure their reward and recognition initiatives are aligned with the strategic intent of the firm. If your reward and recognition efforts aren't supporting where the company is headed, you're simply not going to get there. These are the elements of the model:

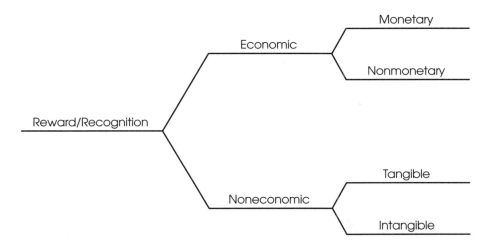

Types of reinforcers

- Economic monetary reinforcers—base salary, salary increases, bonuses, fringe benefits, commissions, spiffs; anything that comes in the form of dollars

- Economic nonmonetary reinforcers—merchandise awards of significant dollar value, such as an incentive trip, new car, plasma TV with surround sound; something that is of a significant dollar value but does not take the form of money

- Noneconomic tangibles—a better work area, plaques, hats, jackets, T-shirts, group pizza lunches, merchandise certificates; any reward that is tangible in nature and that the recipient would consider to have moderate economic value

- Noneconomic intangibles—motivational feedback, praise, a certificate of achievement, an invitation to lunch, acknowledgment at a sales meeting or in a corporate publication; something that is not tangible in nature and has no real economic value

Economic monetary reinforcers. Monetary rewards are of high value to most salespeople—but to be truly effective, they must be clearly aligned with your goals. Financial rewards should be used to reinforce specifically the kind of behavior that leads to the desired results. Although monetary reward is not the only—or even always the best—way to reinforce improved behavior from salespeople, it does send a signal that the culture in your team is changing and that the goals and expectations you have set are important.

Economic nonmonetary reinforcers. One reason nonmonetary incentive awards can be especially useful in turbulent times—better than cash, in fact—is that they raise the level of awareness of sales behaviors that need changing immediately, and unlike cash incentives, they carry a lasting recognition value. Every time someone notices the plasma TV a rep was awarded or the snapshots from her trip to Hawaii, it reinforces the behavior that resulted in the award. Using nonmonetary awards also allows you to offer a variety incentives, so you can appeal to a wide range of reps' interests—and as we saw in chapter 5, reinforcement works only when the individual perceives it as positive.

> Better than cash, nonmonetary incentive awards raise the level of awareness of sales behaviors that need changing immediately.

Nonmonetary incentive programs should meet the SMART criteria:

- Specific—Make the rules for winning specific, clear, and easily understood.

- Measurable—Base the award on a measurable sales metric.

- Achievable—Offer a greater number of smaller awards more often rather than just one big award.

- Results oriented—Make sure you're rewarding the right result for your business.

- Timely—Time your incentive program so it doesn't clash with other important activities in your company.

Both economic nonmonetary reinforcers and noneconomic tangible reinforcers (the middle two branches in the previous figure) should take into account the concept of trophy value. Part of the value of winning the Stanley Cup is the award ceremony. Somehow, it just wouldn't seem the same if someone said, "Nice game, guys. You should be receiving the Cup via common carrier in about ten days. Naturally, it will be insured."

I've been involved in several custom-designed leadership development programs developed by Korn/Ferry Leadership and Talent Consulting. Portions of these programs were conducted at the U.S. Olympic Training Center. Not only did the participants learn how effective leadership practices parallel effective coaching of Olympians, but they also had lunch and dinner with Olympians, experienced learning some basic skills in an Olympic sport, received a behind-the-scenes tour of the Center, and had the opportunity to purchase shirts, jackets, soccer balls, and other items from the Center's gift shop. I can assure you that each of those had a very high trophy value for the participants—including the 12 or so senior sales managers who were part of the program!

Noneconomic tangible reinforcers. Recognizing performance with noneconomic tangible awards—plaques, jackets, desk sets, reserved parking spaces—is an inexpensive way to reinforce the right behavior in sales reps. Such an award is insignificant in financial terms; certainly the intrinsic value is not enough to motivate a rep to improve, so it works only when combined with other forms of compensation and reward.

> Recognizing performance with noneconomic tangible awards is an inexpensive way to reinforce the right behavior in sales reps.

The power of noneconomic tangible awards comes from what they represent, so these symbolic awards need to be presented with a little pizzazz. In many organizations that understand the value of symbolism, the belief is that the greatest impact comes from "a nickel's worth of award presented with a dollar's worth of recognition."

Noneconomic intangible reinforcers. These intangibles—a pat on the back, a congratulatory e-mail, a nod and a smile—involve social reinforcement of both results and behaviors. Such simple, mostly cost-free gestures are powerful reinforcers, because once a rep's basic economic requirements are met, psychological income—a feeling of competence, self-worth, and self-confidence—often becomes more important.

There are solid numbers to back this up. A recent McKinsey survey report titled "Motivating People" showed that that economic incentives do work to motivate people: 60 percent of people are highly motivated by a performance-based bonus. But what may surprise you is that an even greater number of people get that same motivational effect from motivational feedback. In fact, 67 percent say they find their manager's praise and acknowledgment to be highly motivating. Other noneconomic intangibles are almost as effective: 63 percent find attention from leaders highly motivating, and 62 percent respond to opportunities to lead projects or task forces. These outstrip the next-best monetary reinforcers: 52 percent find an increase in base salary highly motivating, whereas just 35 percent get the same motivating effect from stock or stock options.

> Once a rep's basic economic requirements are met, psychological income—a feeling of competence, self-worth, and self-confidence—often becomes more important.

People also aspire to be part of something important and meaningful. This is why celebrations and recognition ceremonies can be valuable reinforcers. Celebrating success reaffirms to your reps that they are headed in the right direction. In tough times, most companies scale back their celebrations or cancel them altogether—but it is worth remembering that these celebrations don't have to be expensive to be effective. For instance, in one company, to recognize the work of customer service staff, the managers and field service people worked the customer-service desks and phones while the reps were treated to a catered luncheon and recognition ceremony.

Recognition is also vital because numerous surveys show that no company can have loyal customers without fully engaged employees who care about and are excited about what they're doing. If your sales reps don't have a positive image of your company, your customers won't, either.

When it comes to the four elements of reward and recognition described above, three things are critical:

1. Alignment.

2. Alignment.

3. Alignment.

If senior leadership wants X, dollars are being given to reps for Y, and you're delivering motivational feedback for Z, you'll find that three things will happen:

1. Senior leadership will be unhappy.

2. You'll be unhappy.

3. Your sale reps will not only be unhappy, they will be driven slowly nuts by the conflicting messages.

Don't let that happen. Make sure there is 100 percent alignment on every dimension.

Use These Tools at Home, Too

One of the most frequent comments our instructors get after a workshop on the ideas outlined in this book is "I wish I'd had this workshop before we raised the kids." Indeed, you should integrate the tools into your home life. These principles don't start and stop at your office doorway; the more you use expectations, accountability, and feedback, the more they become just the way you do things naturally. You now have the power to change many lives for the better, including your family's.

> These principles don't start and stop at your office doorway. You now have the power to change many lives for the better.

I helped the parents of a boy, Ben, who was flunking out of school. He was at a private school, his third school in two years, and if he didn't show significant improvement in the next six-week marking period, he would not be readmitted in the fall.

First Ben's parents sat down for a discussion like the one described in chapter 7 on developmental feedback. They avoided personal criticism ("Ben, how come you're so dumb in math?") and used future-oriented, open-ended, neutral questions that focused on grades (e.g., "How could we get your math grades up?"). They communicated positive expectations, separating Ben from his behavior and grades by using statements such as "We know you're better than you're doing," while still holding him accountable for his grades.

Just as shorter goal-setting cycles are helpful for sales reps who are in trouble, they can help kids in trouble at school, so Ben and his parents started setting weekly goals. Without informational feedback, the weekly goals would not have been effective, so Ben's parents sent his teachers a quick e-mail each week asking them to assign Ben a grade. His parents reinforced Ben every time his grades improved and when he studied or spent extra time on his homework.

Seven weeks later, Ben's average grade was D-plus. That might not sound like much, but it was a significant improvement, and it meant he would be readmitted in the fall. I'd like to be able to tell you that Ben is now a straight-A student, but he's not. He is, however, a good, solid C-plus student who recently entered his senior year in a public high school.

The tools can also be applied at home to reduce another common concern for parents: fighting between siblings. A woman named Ashley approached me during a coffee break at a workshop and told me that for the past year her two children—Brian and Cindy—had been fighting more than normal. I asked her: "When do the kids get more attention—when they fight, or when they're good?" She answered—slapping her forehead at the same time—that she and her husband, Bob, tended to ignore the kids as long as they were behaving but gave them lots of attention when they were fighting. They were—through attention—reinforcing the bad behavior rather than the good behavior.

> The tools can also be applied at home to reduce another common concern for parents: fighting between siblings.

Ashley and Bob implemented the tools of expectation, accountability, and feedback. When the kids were fighting, they told them that fighting was not acceptable behavior in their household. Let's say this equals one unit of attention. Then they made sure that when Brian and Cindy were not fighting they received two or three units of attention. The children were reinforced with comments like "I'm glad to see the two of you getting along so well," with an occasional tangible reinforcer tied in, such as an ice cream cone when they were playing well together.

Spread These Ideas Throughout Your Company

The ideas we've been discussing have been used to improve performance and results in every aspect of business, because all people, no matter what field they work in, respond to expectations, accountability, and feedback. Encourage colleagues in other departments at your firm to introduce these techniques, because they will work there, too. Lend your book to your boss, the director of manufacturing, your distribution head, and directors of marketing, customer service, research and development, and so on, throughout your company. Although the content is directed primarily at you as a sales manager, the tools and techniques are applicable in—and have been used by—every functional area in the business, health care, government, and military worlds.

Communication within and between departments, teamwork, and human relations will improve wherever these tools are implemented. They can also be used by other departments in any industry to improve specific non-sales metrics. For instance, in

> These tools can be used by other departments in any industry to improve specific non-sales metrics.

manufacturing, they can be used to improve productivity or scrap rate; in a hospital, staff turnover; in an educational institution, average grades or the number of students who graduate.

Seven Reasons to Start Now

Let's wrap up by going back to chapter 1 and looking at some results I briefly mentioned and promised to come back to. In each instance, the results come from a sales manager putting to work the tools you've just learned.

The sales manager whose reps "are getting exceptional results in a tough market." You remember Rick, from the first paragraph in the first chapter? Rick and the six examples below used virtually all the tools in this book. But Rick, like the others, found that several tools stood out as being particularly useful.

1. Rick reported that his reps particularly made progress when he acknowledged current reality and then created a new reality. Rick had been trying to pump everyone up, saying "We can do it," but hadn't gone through the process of working with his reps to lay out exactly where they were. It was a tough market, and they hadn't really examined the market in detail, so the "pumping-up" was seen as a bunch of arm waving that was in denial of what was really going on. Once Rick acknowledged how tough things were and then said, "We have the skills and capabilities to get through this with flying colors," things began to change.

2. As part of his workshop analysis, Rick found—as do most sales managers—that he was extinguishing improvements by hopping on any downward drift while ignoring all the upticks. With this new awareness, he began using developmental feedback individually with each rep to jump-start sales, reinforcing every uptick he could find, ignoring small drops in performance, and applying more developmental feedback only for significant drops.

3. Rick also found he was out of balance—overdoing accountability and underdoing support—which he immediately rebalanced.

Increased average line items per order from 6 to 11.2 on the inside order desk in a little under two weeks. Here are the most useful things the sales manager did in that situation:

1. Changed the informational feedback cycle. Calls came in all day long, so there were plenty of opportunities for those on the inside order desk to increase average line items by suggesting related items or mentioning the daily or weekly specials. But the information was being shared only once a month. The informational feedback cycle was shortened to daily and then, at the request of the reps, to hourly.

2. Changed the informational feedback format. Previously, it had been given as a single number—e.g., "This past month we averaged 6.1 line items per order. We need to get that up." This was changed to a graph format; inside reps could look at a combined-average graph to see how the whole team was doing and their own individual graphs to check their personal numbers.

3. Reinforced every improvement for the first four to five weeks. In two weeks, the results hit 11.2, bobbed around a little bit, and ended up at the 11.2 average. When it was clear their average had stabilized at 11.2, the reinforcement schedule was changed to intermittent.

Increased sales of higher-margin products. Although there are numerous examples of such increases reported in program results, I've picked just one to describe. Here are the three most important steps the company took:

1. Changed from dollar volume goals to gross margin dollar goals.

2. Created a system that provided each rep a weekly graph of that rep's gross margin dollars for the week, a weekly graph of the team's gross margin dollars, and monthly graphs of the other sales metrics they were accountable for.

3. Stepped up the reinforcement schedule to make sure that the positive-to-negative feedback ratio was at least 3:1. Any time a rep improved gross margin dollars, he was reinforced. If all team members improved gross margin dollars, all were acknowledged as a team.

In this particular instance, sales reps were on a base salary with a small commission. Gross margin dollars grew 53 percent over the next six months.

Increased unit sales by 15 percent while maintaining the same average gross margin. In this situation, the company saw an opportunity to gain market share. These are the three most important actions they learned and implemented:

1. Moved informational feedback from monthly to weekly and put it in graph form.

2. Reinforced every upward tick in unit sales where the rep maintained the same average gross margin or better.

3. Used developmental feedback when gross margin slipped—e.g., "Jon, I see that while your unit sales are up, your gross margin has slipped by a point and a half. What can we do to keep unit sales growing without cutting our gross margin?"

Increased sales on targeted lines by 200 percent. In this initiative, the company took about seven weeks to reach the 200 percent mark. Here's what was found most important:

1. The sales manager acknowledged that it was an audacious goal for the current market conditions and suggested they set two goals: one they were fairly sure they were going to reach, and another goal of 200 percent that would incur no penalties but to which everyone would pledge full involvement and commitment.

2. Every time a rep became discouraged, the sales manager used developmental feedback questions to get things back on track—"How do you think we could get there?" "What do you think might be the best next step?"

3. There was reinforcement for effort (that is, for appropriate behavior), lots of reinforcement for any improvements in metrics, and random pizzas, T-shirts, and gift certificates, the awarding of which was surrounded with lots of hoopla.

Generated substantial volume in new accounts. In this situation, a high-performing sales rep accepted a challenge to call on five key accounts being supplied by a competitor. He captured three of the five, which added $2.5 million in new sales. Here is what worked in that case:

1. The sales manager used a form of developmental feedback right out of the box. He went to the rep, named the five accounts he'd like to get switched, and asked, "What do you think would be the best way to go about this?" thinking there would be a discussion between them. The rep looked at the sales manager and said, "Let me see if I've got this right. You want me to switch accounts A, B, C, D, and E? That's a lot." The sales manager nodded. The rep

smiled and said, "Well, you've got the right guy. Let's look at them one by one." Which they did.

2. They constructed a version of the matrix shown in chapter 6 that fit their industry.

3. The choice of when to call in with a progress report was left up to the rep. Whenever he reported on his progress—which was the only time he called in regarding these five accounts—he got lots of reinforcement. It took him 120 days to switch the three accounts.

Reduced credits as a percent of sales from 0.86 percent to 0.74 percent (net annualized savings of $176,000). The sales manager in this situation had exerted generalized pressure over credits but had never set specific targets for them. After our workshop:

1. He talked with each rep about the need to reduce credits, and he set high-low targets to accomplish this objective.

2. Credits were measured weekly, and any improvement was reinforced.

3. One rep wasn't making much progress, so the sales manager used developmental feedback to get things back on track.

Because the reps didn't want to lose the business of any accounts, they had not previously paid much attention to credits. Now they paid careful attention, and even more attention to how they dealt with them. Credits were reduced from 0.86 percent to 0.74 percent, with no loss in volume.

The Bottom Line: Does This Stuff Work?

It sure does. You know best which parts will move your sales volume needle the quickest. What you're after is the kind of behavior change from your reps that raises performance. Although these tools will give your sales a quick boost, be assured that they work well at engineering the behavior change you need from your reps over the long term, in any kind of economic environment. Make these tools part of your day-to-day work, and you will see sustained improvement from your reps.

So that's it. Join the very best and start boosting sales now.

Three Powerful Ways to Accelerate, Deepen, and Sustain the Use of These Three Proven Tools

The content and examples of boosting sales you just read about come from what was originally a two-and-a-half-day workshop. Refined and honed over the past 24 years, this program can now be delivered by culturally knowledgeable facilitators in virtually every country of the world.

Because they all directly influence revenue, the groups for which the program is most applicable include—but are not limited to—field sales managers, complex and branch managers in the financial services field, retail store managers and their direct reports, branch managers in industries such as wholesale distribution, and individuals in the operations segment of restaurants. Here are the three most frequent requests from those who want to go beyond a book:

1. Keynote or Half-Day Presentation

Tom or one of his associates can deliver a powerful keynote or half-day presentation. Sometimes this is a session just for sales managers immediately before or after a sales meeting. Sometimes it's a stand-alone meeting for sales managers, branch managers, complex managers, or operations managers. Other times it's for a senior leadership team. However the scheduling works out, a presentation on Turbulent Times Leadership can make a significant contribution to a strong bottom line.

2. One-to-Two-Day Seminar or Workshop

With a global network of 67 trainers and coaches, this content can be tailored and quickly delivered in multiple locations and multiple languages. At the completion of the program, each sales manager leaves with a detailed blueprint that will significantly shift sales rep behavior and directly impact sales performance.

The seminar or workshop is frequently paired with 90 days of follow-on coaching by certified coaches that ensure project success. The results you read about in the book came from this program. The tools work because they're based not on opinion but on solid research and testing, and because each element has been tested in the crucible of the marketplace and has been proven to automatically trigger a positive response whenever it's used properly.

3. Virtual Learning

Some firms use a virtual learning platform to deliver programs such as this. Doing it right is not cheap, but it can deliver significant value and cost savings over time. There are a number of ways to partner with you, ranging from tailoring and licensing the materials for your use to building a custom-designed program for you.

Read more about option one at www.tomconnellan.com and more about option two at www.salesmanagementtraining.com. Call 800-344-5417 regarding any option. There's more below about what people say about the first two options.

Who's a Sales Manager?

A reasonable question at this point would be "Who's a sales manager?" Rick—described on page one—works for a Fortune 500 firm and would easily be considered a sales manager because he has 12 field sales reps working for him, each of whom is tasked with generating revenue for the company.

But there are countless other individuals with *different* titles who also manage people who generate revenue. The metrics used might be slightly different from those listed on page 29, but the core task of generating revenue is the same. For example:

- In financial services, complex managers and branch managers oversee financial advisors/consultants, and the core metrics in that industry that track profitable revenue include assets under management and return on assets.

- In retail, store managers and department heads oversee the retail operation, and they generally use some version of average basket size as a revenue metric.

- In restaurants—from quick service to full service—some form of average ticket size and daily/weekly sales volume are common revenue metrics that are monitored.

In today's turbulent and highly competitive marketplace, we're in the era of Sales Management 3.0, which I define as "having a direct line of sight to individuals who directly generate or influence revenue." This means that whatever their titles, the three categories of managers described above are engaged in the practice of sales management. Historically, they've never been thought of as sales managers; their job title is usually not sales manager; and neither their job preparation nor their ongoing training typically involves giving them sales management tools and techniques.

Functionally, however, they are sales managers.

So whatever your title and whatever the titles of those who report to you, if you're a 3.0 Sales Manager, this workshop—like this book—is for you.

The Bottom Line

If you want to make the sales manager's job easier and significantly boost sales performance within 30 days, one of these programs is for you. Why? Well, you can judge for yourself, because here's what others say who have had Tom address their group on this topic:

GREAT CONTENT WITH AWESOME DELIVERY!

"What a great general session. Not many people can combine great content with awesome delivery, but you do it with exquisite finesse. Thanks for an outstanding session that delivered actionable ideas in an easy-to-digest manner."

Chief Imagination Officer
The Sales & Marketing Magic Companies

PROFOUND IMPACT!

"Well, you did it again! As I said in my introduction, your leadership training session has been one of the most memorable events in my management career—in addition to having a profound impact on my personal life. I truly believe in the power of your three factors and their impact on associate engagement and productivity. Thanks for another great session."

Co-President
ADP Brokerage Services

THOUGHT PROVOKING!

"All I can say is GREAT JOB! The feedback on the leadership session has all been very positive. Comments like 'Terrific,' 'Best session yet,' and 'Something we can take back to the field and use immediately' were common. What you did in four hours was terrific, and the impact on the group was all positive and thought provoking. Thanks again!"

Vice President
The Home Depot

ABSOLUTE HIT!

"Your leadership workshop was the absolute hit of our conference. As I'm sure you realized, our members are an outgoing and quick-thinking group of company owners and top executives. You held their interest in the palm of your hand, and the only downside was that your session came to an end."

Chairman
The Builder Marketing Society

EXTRAORDINARY!

"Thank you for your extraordinary training! Every time I've put the keys to work, they boost sales productivity. Every time!"

Managing Director
Principal Financial Group

EXCEPTIONAL!

"Exceptional content and exceptional delivery. I came with high expectations, and even those were exceeded. If you have even one underperforming rep on your team, here's where you'll find immediate solutions."

National Sales Manager
Tarkett, Inc.

REAL BENEFITS!

"You had a tough act to follow from our initial Executive SPECS program, but I am happy to report without trepidation or equivocation that you rose to the challenge. Everyone I talked to complimented your presentation and the real benefits they will be able to integrate into their professional and personal lives."

Publisher/Editor
Chain Store Age

EXCELLENCE PERSONIFIED!

"Your session was excellence personified—delivering real hands-on tools and techniques I can use. One of the best leadership programs I have attended."

Vice President
JC Penny

GREAT ROI!

"Wow! Our sales managers report that your tools and techniques are delivering significant results to our bottom line. Your combination of original research and street-smart application produces a great ROI. You're certainly not cheap, but you're very good. Thanks for the great work."

Director of Commercial Sales
GLE Division of Gordon Food Service

See www.tomconnellan.com or call 800-344-5417 for more details on any of the three options for delivering the tools in this book to your sales managers.

Have Tom Keynote Your Next Sales Meeting

Creating Exceptional Customer Experiences

This presentation shows sales reps why customers are tougher today and what you need to do about it right away. It's tied in part to Tom's *Wall Street Journal* bestseller, *Inside the Magic Kingdom,* which describes how Disney creates exceptional customer experiences and how you can do the same.

His basic premise about brands and customers is that "a brand does not and cannot exist separately from your customer's experience." As Tom puts it, "your customer's experience is your brand!"

Participants see how creating an exceptional customer experience builds both a winning brand and a winning bottom line. They learn the five different levels of loyalty and what it takes to move customers from one to the next.

Tom takes you behind the scenes at companies that create world-class customer experiences. He combines that with the latest research to show you how to capture the hearts and minds of your customers. He and his partners have conducted research covering more than 110,000 customer transactions.

One important point Tom brings to your meeting from those 110,000 transactions is the critical employee satisfaction → customer satisfaction → profitability link.

Key points Tom covers include:

- Why, in the eyes of your customer, your competition isn't who you might think it is, and what to do about that.

- How to capitalize on the one internal factor that stands out above all others as the largest single predictor of customer loyalty.

- Why customer satisfaction is a poor predictor of loyalty, and what to do about that.

To read comments from sales executives who have had Tom keynote a sales meeting, and to see a video preview of this presentation, visit his website at www.tomconnellan.com.

About Tom Connellan

When companies like Marriott, FedEx, and Neiman Marcus want to take their performance to another level, they all turn to one man—Tom Connellan. And with good reason. He's solid. Ever year, he keynotes scores of meetings.

A former program director at the Michigan Business School, Tom brings depth and breadth to your conference. Tom has worked in manufacturing and sales. As a company founder and former CEO, he knows firsthand what it takes to grow a business.

He started a service company in the health care field and built it into a network of 1,200 instructors serving 300 hospitals and most of the Fortune 500 firms. More than 1 million participants went through its programs, and two different Surgeon General reports cited the firm's program quality. Tom knows what it's like to be on the firing line of business, because he's been there.

A *New York Times* bestselling author, Tom has nine books and numerous articles to his credit. He's been the editorial director of four management and human resource magazines, a first-level supervisor, and a company president. Tom brings solid content and a passionate delivery style to his presentations. He captures the audience's attention and holds it from start to finish.

Because his keynotes are packed with actionable ideas, everyone leaves Tom's sessions with practical how-to's they can put to work the next day.

For information on schedule and availability, write to 1163 South Main, PMB 306, Chelsea, MI 48118; call 734-428-1580; or visit Tom online at www.tomconnellan.com.

Acknowledgments

Every author says, "I couldn't have done this alone," and every author who's not crazy really means that, because this is where we get to thank those who contributed to our book. For me, it's always a tough job, because there are so many that I always worry about leaving someone out.

So, here goes.

To my good friend and colleague Herb Cohen, who introduced me to the concept of firstborn performance differences, a big thank you. In addition, a big thank you for the friendship and fun over the years, including roping in Ellen at LaGuardia. Thank you, Herb.

Svetlana Ivanova, M.D., Ph.D., Kirti Kalidas, M.D., N.D., and Paula Noack, L.M.T., C.T., all—through their solid approach to integrative medicine—put heartfelt energy into the book. Thanks to each of you.

My program manager, Karen Revill, kept the office running smoothly in spite of the fact that keeping me heading in the right direction while I'm writing must be akin to herding cats. Thank you, Karen.

Cody Kennedy and Jaci Dodd gave me support and advice for every word and were available most any hour of most any day when I needed guidance on a phrase or word. Thank you, Cody and Jaci.

The editing and layout team of Vanessa Mickan and Jeff Morris did a great job of developing, editing, pulling together, and laying out the words you read in this book. Any deficiency is my responsibility; any clarity is theirs. Thank you, Vanessa and Jeff. Thanks as well to Deborah Costenbader for her thorough and diligent proofreading, and to Linda Webster for the excellent index.

Michele DeFilippo of 1106 Design did a great job on the dust jacket and promotional materials for the book. Special thanks to Michele and her entire team. Thank you, Michele.

Amy Collins McGregor's deep book industry knowledge and savvy marketing knowledge have proven to be invaluable. Many thanks to Amy and the entire team at The Cadence Group. Thank you, Amy.

And finally, last but most certainly not least, to Pam Dodd, my patient wife, who—for the most part—tolerated the travails of pulling this book together, my thanks, love, and appreciation. Thank you, Pam.

Index

Accountability
action plan backing up goal, 40–42
activities labeled as goals, 33–34
agreement on metric but not actual goal,
30–32
agreement on metric but pushing goal,
32–33
automatic rubber band effect, 38–40
for children, 3, 113–114
dilution of, 30–43
for firstborns, 3
and goals generally, 7–8
goals not balanced against tradeoffs, 34–35
high goal/low goal flip-flop, 7–8, 35–38
interrelationships among feedback, positive
expectations and
length of goal setting period, 42–43
list of sales metrics, 29–30
sales managers' role in, 6, 7–8
sliding scale approach to, 39–40
"standard-goal" approach, 37–38
Action plans, 40–42
Activities labeled as goals, 33–34
Aptitude versus attitude, 11–12
Automatic rubber band effect, 38–40
Awards. *See* Reward and recognition programs

Behavior
change of sales reps' behaviors, 102–104
developmental feedback on, 90–91
examples of, 104
nonbehaviors versus, 103–104
reinforcement of, 69–71, 73
Behavioral engineering
changing reps' behaviors, not attitude or
motivation, 102–104
changing sales managers' behaviors,
104–105
interrelationships among accountability,
feedback and positive expectations, 105
metrics and, 104
nonbehaviors and, 103–104
toughness of sales managers, 105–106
Belief in sales reps. *See* Positive expectations

Body language
body position, 19–20, 21
eyes, 21
facial expressions, 21
gestures, 20–21
head movements, 21
in personal zone, 24
positive expectations and, 16, 19–22, 26–27
in public zone, 24–25
in social zone, 24
Body position, 19–20, 21

Checkpoints in action plan, 41
Children
feedback for, 4, 113–114
fighting between siblings, 114
goals for, 113
IQ of, 10–11
positive expectations of, 3, 10–11, 113–114
research on firstborns, 3–4
responsibility and accountability for, 3,
113–114
school performance of, 113–114
Cold shoulder, 19–20
Comfort zone, 69
Communication. *See also* Developmental feedback; Feedback; Informational feedback;
Motivational feedback
body language, 16, 19–22, 26–27
emotional content of, 16–17
interruptions in, 17, 25–26
of positive expectations, 16–28
vocal intonation of, 16, 18–19, 26, 27
words of message, 16–18, 26, 27
Contingency plans, 41–42
Continuous reinforcement of new behaviors,
64–67
Credits, reduction in, 7, 118
Customer responses to sales reps, 78–81

Developmental feedback. *See also* Feedback
asking for solutions using right questions,
91–93
closing the deal, 96–99

defining issue factually, 90–91
definition of, 8, 47
examples of, 49–50, 117–118
exploring options, 93–95
follow up after, 98–99
negative feedback versus, 87–88
positive expectations from, 98
preparation for, 88–90
reinforcement of positive responses to, 95–96
"Sandwich Interview" for, 99
summarizing discussion and proposing a goal, 96–98
summary on, 88, 99–100

Economic monetary reinforcers, 59, 109–110
Economic nonmonetary reinforcers, 109, 110–111
Environment for positive expectations
    interruptions, 17, 25–26
    proximity, 17, 23–25, 27
    setting, 17, 22–23, 27
Environmental factors for high performers, 4–8. See also Accountability; Feedback; Positive expectations
Errors of sales reps, 54–55
Excellence, reinforcement of, 61–62
Expectations. See Positive expectations
Extinction, 47–48, 50–52, 115
Eyes
    positive expectations and, 21
    proximity and, 24

Facial expressions
    positive expectations and, 21
    proximity and, 24
Feedback. See also Developmental feedback; Informational feedback; Motivational feedback
    for children, 4, 113–114
    for firstborns, 4
    interrelationships among accountability, positive expectations and, 105
    meanings of, 45
    negative feedback (punishment), 46, 48, 50, 52–55, 72–73
    no feedback (extinction), 46, 47–48, 50–52, 115
    pitfalls of extinction and punishment, 50–55

positive-to-negative feedback ratio of 3:1, 72–73, 116
request by sales reps for more feedback, 55
sales managers' role in, 6, 8
"shoot the messenger" syndrome, 53–54
types of, 8, 46–47
Firstborns
    feedback for, 4
    as higher performers, 2–5
    positive expectations for, 3
    responsibility and accountability for, 3
    5-90-5 ratio on sales reps, 107–108
Follow up after developmental feedback, 98–99
Future-oriented questions, 91–92

Gestures
    positive expectations and, 20–21
    proximity and, 24–25
Goals. See also Accountability
    action plans for, 40–42
    activities labeled as, 33–34
    agreement on metric but not actual goal, 30–32
    agreement on metric but pushing goal, 32–33
    automatic rubber band effect, 38–40
    for children, 113
    developmental feedback and, 96–98
    Gotta Get/Gonna Shoot For approach to, 37–38
    high goal/low goal flip-flop, 7–8, 35–38
    inappropriate goals, 7–8
    informational feedback and, 76–78, 84
    length of goal setting period, 42–43, 77
    min-max approach to, 37–38
    not balanced against tradeoffs, 34–35
    probability of success versus degree of motivation, 35–36
    "standard-goal" approach, 37–38
    stretch goals, 38–40
    terminology referring to, 33
    tough goals, 106
Gotta Get/Gonna Shoot For approach to goals, 37–38
Graphs for informational feedback, 83–85, 116

Hand gestures
    positive expectations and, 20–21
    proximity and, 24–25

HAPs ("high aptitude personnel"), 11–12
Head movements, positive expectations and, 21
"High aptitude personnel" (HAPs), 11–12
High goal/low goal flip-flop, 7–8, 35–38
High performers
    environmental factors for, 4–8
    firstborns as, 2–5
    research and statistics on, 2–6

Immediate feedback, 60–61, 82–83
Improvements, reinforcement of, 61–62, 69
Informational feedback. *See also* Feedback
    access to sales metrics, 75
    as competitive, 85
    definition of, 8, 47
    examples of, 49, 116, 117
    goals and, 76–78, 84
    graphs for, 83–85, 116
    immediate feedback, 82–83
    positive metrics and, 78–82
    relevancy of, 78
    request for more feedback, 55
    sales calls and, 78–81
    as simple, 84
    as specific, 84
    summary on, 76, 85–86
Intelligence, 10–11
Intermittent versus continuous reinforcement,
    64–67
Interruptions, 17, 25–26
Intimate zone, 23
Intonation. *See* Vocal intonation
IQ, 10–11

Jacobson, Lenore, 10–11

King, Albert S., 11–12
Korn/Ferry Leadership and Talent Consulting,
    111

Line graphs, 84–85
Livingston, J. Sterling, 12–13
Low goal/high goal flip-flop, 7–8, 35–38

Managers. *See* Sales managers
McKinsey survey report on motivation,
    111–112
Metrics. *See also* Informational feedback
    action plan for goals, 40–42

agreement on metric but not actual goal,
    30–32
agreement on metric but pushing goal,
    32–33
behavioral engineering and, 104
list of sales metrics, 29–30, 104
positive versus negative metrics, 78–82
sales reps' access to, 75
Min-max approach to goals, 37–38
Monetary reinforcers, 59, 109–110
Motivational feedback
    adaptation of, to situation and people
        involved, 58–59
    of behavior versus results, 69–73
    continuous versus intermittent reinforce-
        ment, 64–67
    definition of, 8, 46, 48–49
    examples of, 49, 117
    immediate reinforcement, 60–61
    of improvement, not just excellence, 61–62,
        69
    monetary reinforcers, 59, 109–110
    naturally occurring reinforcers, 65–67, 73
    positive-to-negative feedback ratio of 3:1,
        72–73, 116
    principles of positive reinforcement, 60–73
    psychological income as, 59–60
    as reinforcement, 48–49, 57
    request for more feedback, 55
    reward and recognition programs, 52,
        108–113
    ripple effect of, 67–69
    sales managers' approach to reinforcement,
        58
    specific reinforcement, 63–64
    summary on, 60, 73
    types of reinforcers, 109–112
My Fair Lady, 9

Naturally occurring reinforcers, 65–67, 73
Negative feedback (punishment), 46, 48, 50,
    52–55, 72–73
Neutral questions, 92–93
New accounts, 7, 117–118
No feedback (extinction), 46, 47–48, 50–52,
    115
Nonbehaviors, 103–104
Noneconomic intangible reinforcers, 111–112.
    See also Psychological income

Noneconomic tangible reinforcers, 111
Nonperformance. *See* Developmental feedback
Nonverbal communication. *See* Body language

Open-ended questions, 92
Options and developmental feedback, 93–95

Parenting skills, 113–114. *See also* Children
Personal zone, 23
Placebo effect, 15–16
Planning. *See also* Goals
    action plans, 40–42
    contingency plans, 41–42
Pollyanna thinking versus positive expectations, 14
Positive expectations
    aptitude versus attitude, 11–12
    body language and, 16, 19–22, 26–27
    of children, 3, 10–11, 113–114
    communication of, 16–28
    from developmental feedback, 98
    environment involving, 22–28
    for firstborns, 3
    "high aptitude personnel" (HAPs) and, 11–12
    interrelationships among accountability, feedback and, 105
    interruptions and, 17, 25–26
    IQ of children and, 10–11
    message involving, 16–22, 26–28
    placebo effect and, 15–16
    positive thinking versus, 14
    proximity and, 17, 23–25, 27
    Pygmalion Effect, 9, 12–13
    research on, 3, 10–13
    sales managers' role in, 6, 7
    setting and, 17, 22–23, 27
    vocal intonation involving, 16, 18–19, 26, 27
    wishful thinking versus, 13–14
    words involving, 16–18, 26, 27
Positive feedback. *See* Reinforcement
Positive thinking versus positive expectations, 14
Positive-to-negative feedback ratio of 3:1, 72–73, 116
Proximity, 17, 23–25, 27
Psychological income, 59–60. *See also* Noneconomic intangible reinforcers
Public zone, 23–24

Punishment, 48, 50, 52–55, 72–73
Pygmalion Effect, 9, 12–13

Questions for developmental feedback, 91–93

Recognition programs. *See* Reward and recognition programs
Reduced credits, 7, 118
Reinforcement
    adaptation of, to situation and people involved, 58–59
    of behavior versus results, 69–73
    comfort zone and, 69
    continuous reinforcement of new behaviors, 64–67
    definition of motivational reinforcement, 8, 46, 48–49
    economic monetary reinforcers, 59, 109–110
    economic nonmonetary reinforcers, 109, 110–111
    examples, 49, 117
    face-to-face reinforcement, 61
    immediate reinforcement, 60–61
    of improvement, not just excellence, 61–62, 69
    intermittent reinforcement of good habits, 64–67
    monetary reinforcers, 59, 109–110
    motivational feedback as, 48–49, 57
    naturally occurring reinforcers, 65–67, 73
    noneconomic intangible reinforcers, 111–112
    noneconomic tangible reinforcers, 111
    of positive responses to developmental feedback, 95–96
    positive-to-negative feedback ratio of 3:1, 72–73, 116
    principles of positive reinforcement, 60–73
    psychological income as, 59–60
    reward and recognition programs, 52, 108–113
    ripple effect of, 67–69
    roller-coaster pattern and, 68–69
    sales managers' approach to, 58
    SMART criteria for, 110
    specific reinforcement, 63–64
    summary on, 60, 73
    types of reinforcers, 109–112

Responsibility. *See* Accountability
Results, reinforcement of, 69–73
Reward and recognition programs, 52, 108–113
Ripple effect of reinforcement, 67–69
Roller-coaster pattern, 68–69
Rosenthal, Robert, 10–11
Rubber band effect, 38–40

Sales. *See also* Metrics; Sales managers; Sales reps
   of higher-margin products, 7, 116
   improvements in, 7, 115–118
   increased average line items per order, 7, 116
   increased sales on targeted lines, 7, 117
   increased unit sales, 7, 116–117
   metrics in, 29–30
   new accounts, 7, 117–118
   reduced credits and, 7, 118
Sales managers. *See also* Accountability; Feedback; Positive expectations
   as behavioral engineers, 102–113
   change in behavior of, 104–105
   and 5-90-5 ratio on sales reps, 107–108
   out-of-balance behavior of, 6–7, 116
   Pygmalion Effect and, 12–13
   reasons for use of tools to improve sales reps' performance, 7, 115–118
   reinforcement practices of, 58
   requests for more feedback from, 55
   research and statistics on, 5–7
   responses of, to errors of sales reps, 54–55
   reward and recognition programs used by, 52, 108–113
   spread of ideas to improve sales reps' performance throughout company, 114–115
   summary of tools for improvement of sales reps, 5–8, 101, 105–107
   toughness of, 105–106
Sales reps. *See also* Accountability; Developmental feedback; Feedback; Informational feedback; Motivational feedback; Positive expectations
   access to sales metrics by, 75
   behavior change for, 102–104
   customer responses to, 78–81
   errors of, 54–55
   5-90-5 ratio on, 107–108
   nonbehaviors of, 103–104

   request for more feedback by, 55
   reward and recognition programs for, 52, 108–113
   summary of factors for improvement of, 5–8, 101, 105–107
"Sandwich Interview," 99
Seating
   for conference in manager's office, 25
   at conference table, 23
Self-fulfilling prophecy, 7. *See also* Positive expectations
Setting for communication of positive expectations, 17, 22–23, 27
Shaw, George Bernard, 9
"Shoot the messenger" syndrome, 53–54
Sliding scale approach to accountability, 39–40
SMART criteria for reinforcers, 110
Social zone, 23
Solutions and developmental feedback, 91–93
Specific feedback, 63–64, 84
"Standard-goal" approach, 37–38. *See also* Goals
Stretch goals, 38–40
Success versus motivation, 35–36
Supportive feedback. *See* Developmental feedback; Feedback; Informational feedback; Motivational feedback

Toughness, 105–106
Tradeoffs versus goals, 34–35

Underperformance. *See* Developmental feedback

Vocal intonation, 16, 18–19, 26, 27

Wishful thinking versus positive expectations, 13–14